NEW PROFICIENCY ENGLISH

TEACHER'S GUIDE TO BOOK FOUR

W.S. Fowler
J. Pidcock
R. Rycroft

Nelson

Thomas Nelson and Sons Ltd
Nelson House   Mayfield Road
Walton-on-Thames   Surrey
KT12 5PL   UK

51 York Place
Edinburgh
EH1 3JD   UK

Thomas Nelson (Hong Kong) Ltd
Toppan Building 10/F
22A Westlands Road
Quarry Bay   Hong Kong

Distributed in Australia by
Thomas Nelson Australia
480 La Trobe Street
Melbourne   Victoria 3000
and in Sydney, Brisbane, Adelaide and Perth

First published by Thomas Nelson and Sons Ltd 1985

ISBN 0–17–555610–5
NCN 71–ECE–9254–01

Designed by The New Book Factory, London
Phototypeset by Parkway Illustrated Press, London and Abingdon
Printed in Hong Kong

Printed in Great Britain by Dotesios Printers Limited, Wiltshire

Acknowledgements

The publishers wish to thank the following for permission to
use copyright material:
an extract from *Cairo* by James Aldridge, copyright ©
James Aldridge 1969, reproduced by permission of Curtis
Brown Ltd, London (Unit 7, Activity 2); The Sunday
Telegraph for an article by Mary Kenny which appeared in
The Sunday Telegraph of 13 May 1984 (Unit 8, Activity 1);
reprinted by permission of William Heinemann Ltd, an
extract from *The Forties* by Alan Jenkins, copyright ©
A. Jenkins 1977 (Unit 10, Activity 1); reproduced by
permission of Curtis Brown Ltd, London and Jonathan Cape
Ltd, an extract from *The Pendulum Years* by Bernard Levin
(Unit 10, Activity 2); Mitchell Beazley London Ltd for two
tables from the *Mitchell Beazley Encyclopaedia of
Knowledge* (Unit 11, Activity 1); extracts from *Supernature:
an ecology of the occult* and *Lifetide* by Lyall Watson,
copyright © L. Watson 1973 and 1979 respectively,
reprinted by permission of Hodder & Stoughton Ltd
(Unit 13, Activities 1 and 2).

Every effort has been made to trace owners of the
copyright, but if any omissions can be rectified the
publishers will be pleased to make the necessary
arrangements.

Contents

Introduction

Changes in the examination syllabus

New Proficiency English Book 4 covers the areas of Paper 4 Listening Comprehension and Paper 5 Interview in the Cambridge Certificate of Proficiency in English examination and takes into account all the changes proposed in the 1984 syllabus.

The changes can be summed up as follows:

Paper 4: Listening comprehension
1 There will be a series of *recorded* texts.
2 Questions will be of varying kinds, *not limited to multiple choice*, and will make use of a combined question paper/answer sheet.
3 The test will carry a final total of 20 marks out of the whole examination total of 180 marks.
4 The texts will include radio-type sequences, situational dialogues, announcements, etc., and non-standard accents will be used.
5 The use of recorded material signifies a move away from the literature-oriented texts of the 1975 syllabus towards authentic spoken English in a variety of realistic contexts.

Paper 5: Interview
1 The photograph-based conversation has been retained.
2 The reading-aloud exercise has been retained but modified. In the interview the candidate will be given a booklet containing a series of reading passages, asked to look at a particular one, and given a few moments to prepare not only to read it but also to identify the speech situation in which it might occur.
3 The third part contains a variety of possibilities, including role-play, giving definitions or opinions, giving short talks on prepared topics, taking part in discussions, etc., and, if the candidates have been studying the optional texts, discussing (or giving talks about) them. In addition, the third part may be taken either individually or in groups of three, according to the policy of the examination centre.

The design of the course

The four books comprising the *New Proficiency English* course can be used independently to concentrate on a specific paper in the examination, but they have been written in such a way that they relate to each other. We have tried to make this relationship loose enough to avoid monotony, but close enough for students to be able to practise and reinforce any language or skills they have used in the linked units in *Books 1* and *2*.

The table below shows how the 18 teaching units in *Book 4* relate to units in *Books 1* and *2*.

Book 4	Book 1	Book 2
1	1	1
2	2	2
3	4	—
4	5	4
5	6	5
6	8	—
7	10	8
8	11	9
9	12	—
10	13	10
11	15	12
12	16	—
13	17	13
14	19	14
15	20	—
16	21	16
17	23	18
18	24	—

The contents of *Book 4*

Each of the 18 teaching units in *Book 4* (intended to occupy 1½ class hours) is divided into Listening and Speaking sections and contains:

Listening
Pre-listening activity: This is intended to allow students a few minutes to talk in a context related to the listening task that follows.
Activity 1: This is generally a fact-based task.
Activity 2: This is generally longer and more complex than Activity 1, requiring students to gather information by inference or interpretation as well as by straight comprehension.

In the interests of keeping our approach flexible, however, we have not forced all units to follow the same pattern.

Speaking
Questions on the photographs and related topics: Our

experience has taught us that photo contrasts, which we used in the original *First Certificate English Book 5* and *Proficiency English Book 5*, give more food for thought and yield better results in the classroom than single photographs, but in this book we have varied the approach, occasionally using one photograph and occasionally more than two.

Speech situation/Reading aloud: A short passage for reading aloud, linked to the theme of the unit, is followed by questions of the type used in the examination interview.

Structured communication activity: A variety of communicative activities have been included, some requiring individual preparation and some group work. The listening exercises in some units lend themselves to follow-up role-play and other activities.

Finally, there are two test units, which contain material with no thematic link.

Suggested methodology

Listening exercises

As the examination text requires the tape to be played twice only, with suitable pauses beforehand for the students to look over the questions, and after each listening for the answers to be written, we feel that two plays should be the target by the last term of the course, if not before. After all, in real life one rarely gets more than one! However, in view of the fact that this type of recorded material may be new to a large number of students doing a Proficiency course, we would recommend teachers to be flexible at first and adopt the approach 'twice at least but as often as necessary', always *provided that students realise that the point of the exercise is to select the relevant needed information from what they hear and NOT to try and understand every word.* Students should be encouraged to work in pairs or small groups; in this way weaker students are helped and notes can be compared after each listening. They should be allowed a minute or so to look at the task requirements beforehand; and after each listening there should be a pause to give them time to talk about their answers. In the examination listening test, however, the pauses will be briefer; something like 20 seconds for the preparation of the questions, 15 seconds between listenings, and 15 seconds at the end. In our opinion such short pauses should only be used when the tasks are being done individually, as a test.

Questions on the photographs

The best results with the photographs always come when students work in pairs/small groups. Below we list four suggested techniques which help to vary the learning experience with the photographs.

1 In pairs or groups of three or four. One student has the photo (the book open) and the other(s) can't see it. The other(s) is/are allowed 20 questions to guess as exactly as possible what is in the photo. The student with the photo should demand a high degree of precision in the description (i.e. what is in the background/top right-hand corner, etc.) but should not limit him/herself simply to answering yes or no. The best results come when the student with the photo helps the guessers with the occasional question or comment. For this activity it is obviously essential that the guessers should not have had the chance of seeing the photos beforehand.

2 This is an exercise testing memory and powers of observation, and works best if the photo contains a lot of detail. In pairs or small groups. All the students look at the photograph for a short time, and try to take in as much detail as possible. Then, in pairs or groups, one student can see the photo and the other(s) can't. The students who can't see have to rebuild the picture from memory as exactly as they can. Before the exercise begins to drag, the photo should be seen and discussed.

3 Second opinion. This is useful with photo contrasts. In pairs. Instead of both students talking about both photos, each takes a different one and studies it in depth, not only answering any of the questions he/she finds interesting but also building up his/her own short list of questions to ask his/her partner's opinion about. After this brief (5–8 minute) individual stage, the two students get together and work on the photos one by one, talking about their own questions or points that have interested them, (i.e. not slavishly working through our list of questions, which are intended as suggestions only).

4 A second reconstruction exercise, this time with photo contrasts and linked with note-taking. In pairs/small groups. The students look briefly at both photos and take notes individually about their content; they then close their books. They should then write down two or three sentences in which they sum up in their own words what each photo is about, and suggest what the two photos have in common. After this brief (7–10 minute) individual stage, the students work together to compare notes and summaries.

Speech situation/reading aloud

Here are some suggestions for bringing this exercise to life.

1 The students work in pairs to prepare the passage, identify where it comes from, etc.; each student in the pair could read it aloud once. Then the class comes together to compare notes.

2 In pairs. Both students prepare the passage. Then a role-play format is adopted, where one student is an actor/actress 'rehearsing' the passage as if it were lines he/she has to say in a play. The other student is the play director, who makes comments on the 'performance' until every sentence is 'just right'. As well as being enjoyable, this exercise makes both partners aware of the factors involved in good reading.

We recommend 5–8 minutes as a maximum time for this exercise.

Structured communication activity

We feel that with this type of activity many teachers do not give enough attention to helping students develop *accuracy* of expression as well as *fluency*. Students often express discontent because they want to know if they are speaking correctly, but have no way of knowing if the teacher lets everything pass when they are doing relatively free oral exercises. We believe that the following three rules of thumb will help both students and teachers get the best out of this type of activity.

1 Students should be allowed enough time to prepare themselves properly; they should not be rushed into beginning.

2 The teacher needs a sensitive correction strategy. He/she will need to help with lexis/expressions in response to each student's particular needs during the activity, but will cut off the student's fluency if he/she does any more than supply the needed help. The best approach seems to be for the teacher to note down any common and recurring mistakes while the activity is going on, ensuring that the students see that this is being done and know why.

3 Then, armed with these notes and while the activity is still fresh in the students' minds (and in his/her own!) the teacher can use the notes as the basis for some remedial explanation/practice (either at the end of the same class or in the following one). This has the double benefit of (possibly!) putting right some things that the students *know* they have difficulty with, and also of showing that their oral work is given value within the course framework.

It is our hope that this aural/oral book in the *New Proficiency English* series will not only provide Proficiency examination candidates with practice in all the skills they will need in Papers 4 and 5, but that it will also make that practice enjoyable in its own right.

Will Fowler, John Pidcock, Robin Rycroft
Barcelona, July 1984.

Answer key to Listening activities

Unit 1
People

Activity 1
1A; 2D; 3B; 4C

Activity 2
Students should have ticked the following:
4, 5, 7, 9, 10, 12, 13, 14

Unit 2
Work

Activity 1
1 No. 10; 2 No. 8; 3 No. 5; 4 No. 2

Activity 2
True: 4, 7, 9, 10, 11, 12
False: 1, 2, 3, 5, 6, 8

Unit 3
Decoding information

Activity 1

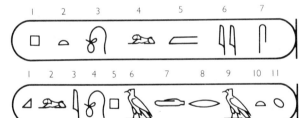

5 Ptolemy
2 Cleopatra

Activity 2
1 Base camp. Radio set up on Saturday.
2 Porter fell on ice. Food load lost down crevasse. Other porters worried.
3 Gale slowed them down.
4 Avalanche fell onto glacier and blocked the way.
5 Small advance camp established Sunday morning. Consolidated Sunday afternoon.
6 Tom and Frank heard strange noise, possibly yeti.
7 Tom and Frank struck camp on Monday for assault on summit.
8 Frank had a fall. Saved by rope on the edge of precipice.
9 Tom and Frank wanted to establish camp late Monday but couldn't.

Unit 4
Processes and procedures

Activity 1
Students should have ticked the following:
1, 3, 4, 6, 8, 10

Activity 2
True: 1, 4, 6
False: 2, 3, 5, 7

Unit 5
News slant

Activity 1
1 An armed dissident group, the Ruritanian Liberation Front, occupied the British Embassy in Semenath, Ruritania.
2 Yesterday morning.
3 Up to 115.
4 They want safe passage by a British Airways plane to the neighbouring state of Sylvania, where they have been offered political asylum.
5 A military dictatorship, which came to power through a coup d'etat two years ago.

Activity 2
True: 3, 5
False: 2, 4, 6, 7

Activity 3
True: 3, 5, 6, 9, 10
False: 1, 2, 4, 7, 8

Unit 6
Schedules

Activity 1
Jim and Sally: A805; Sheffield Road; fair till 2 a.m.; cricket 11.30–6.30, Recreation Ground; zoo 10.00–8.00, Haddon
Eileen and Andrew: A719 or A784; station car park; rock music 6.00–12.00, precinct; showjumping 10.00–2.00/2.45–

5.00, Ring Two; go-karting 10.00–8.00, Haddon
You and Pat: A15, near Burnwell Station; dogs 2.00–4.30,
Ring One (Main Ring); motorcycles 2.00 and 5.00, Ring Two;
showjumping 10.00–2.00/2.45–5.00, Ring Two

Activity 2

Time	Group 1 Scripting/production	Group 2 Technical	Group 3 Acting	Day
09.15–09.30	Welcome address by Alan Drinkall			
09.45–10.45	Introductory session with Gillian Allen			
10.45–11.15	←——— Coffee ———→			
11.15–12.45	'Some production problems – basic theory' by Alan Braine	'Problems with sound and recording' by Ned Grigson	'Drama exercises, mime and movement' led by Pam Taylor	①
13.00–14.00	←——— Lunch ———→			S
14.00–15.30	'Practical problems – scripting direction, production' by Alan Braine and Gillian Allen	'Video – visual aspects and camera use' by Ned Grigson	'On camera' led by Pam Taylor	A T
15.30–16.00	←——— Tea ———→			U R
16.00–18.00	Workshop 'Brainstorm – What programme shall we make?' led by Gillian Allen and Alan Braine	'Coordination of sound/vision' by Ned Grigson	'On camera exercises' led by Pam Taylor	D A Y
18.00–19.00	←——— Free ———→			
19.00–20.00	←——— Dinner ———→			
20.00–22.00	←——— Showing of the film *2010* and discussion ———→			
09.15–10.45	Workshop: 'Scripting, preparing and polishing' led by Gillian Allen and Alan Braine	Workshop: 'Practical technical problems' led by Ned Grigson	Guinea pigs for Technical group practical workshop	
10.45–11.15	←——— Coffee ———→			②
11.15–12.45	←——— Briefing session on script by Scripting group with active participation of Technical and Acting groups ———→			S
13.00–14.00	←——— Lunch ———→			U N
14.00–15.30	←——— 'Filming ———→			D
15.30–16.00	←——— Tea ———→			A Y
16.00–18.30	←——— Editing and mixing ———→			
19.00–20.00	←——— Dinner ———→			
20.00–22.00	←——— Showing of the film and discussion ———→			

Unit 7
Travel

Activity 1

Total number of passengers handled in year: Chicago 45 million; London 27½ million; Georgia 40 million; Los Angeles 33 million

Total number of international passengers: Frankfurt 12 million; New York 13 million; London 23½ million

True: 2, 3, 4
False: 1, 5, 6, 7

Activity 2

True: 1, 3, 4, 5
False: 2, 6

Unit 8
Women in society

Activity 1

1C; 2C; 3B; 4B

Activity 2

True: 3, 4, 5, 8, 10
False: 1, 2, 6, 7, 9

Unit 9
Speeches

Activity 1

Students should have ticked the following:
4, 5, 6, 8, 9, 11

Activity 2

Questions A–D are open questions. No one set of answers is correct.
Students should have ticked the following:
1, 2, 3, 4, 8, 9
6 and 7 are subjective replies. Students should have ticked either 6 or 7 and should be able to explain their reasons for doing so.

Unit 10
The Past

Activity 1 Part 1

Butter:	100g (later 50g) a week
Cheese:	20–25g a week
Eggs:	1 a fortnight; expectant mothers and children under 5, 3 a week.
Tea:	50g a week; more for OAPs
Sugar:	350g a week; more in jam-making season
Sweets:	50g a week
Onions:	None
Bananas:	None
Oranges:	None; except for children

Activity 1 Part 2

True: 1, 3, 4
False: 2, 5

Activity 2

1D; 2A; 3D; 4B

Unit 11
Leisure and education

Activity 1

Sex Women		Age-group covered 20-30	
Category	unmarried	married with no children	married with children
Television	10.7	14.2	19.8
Crafts and hobbies	11.6	18.6	20.7
Gardening	0.3	2.4	3.1
Excursions	7.0	8.4	7.7
Other activities	6.7	9.5	13.6
Walking	5.7	4.3	7.8
Active physical recreation as participant	28.0	15.4	9.8
Reading	7.5	6.1	4.0
Cinema / Theatre going	5.6	2.8	1.4
Club activities	5.3	3.2	1.8
Spectator sports	1.7	1.7	1.0
Visits to pubs	2.9	2.2	2.2
Other social activities	7.0	11.2	7.0

Activity 2

Sex Men		Age-group covered 20-30	
Category	unmarried	married with no children	married with children
Excursions	8.7	8.7	8.7
Spectator sports	2.4	1.7	2.4
Other activities	11.8	8.5	11.8
Television	10.3	13.8	20.8
Gardening	1.3	3.4	6.2
Crafts/hobbies	4.2	5.6	5.6
Maintenance	3.9	10.9	8.8
Walking	2.0	4.8	4.1
Social activities	2.7	4.1	3.4
Reading	6.5	5.6	3.7
Cinema/theatre-going	3.3	2.6	1.2
Club activities	6.4	2.9	4.3
Active physical recreation as participant	24.2	22.1	15.1
Visits to pubs	12.3	5.3	3.9

Unit 12
Advertisements

Activity 1
1st fl. flt.:   ground floor, not first floor
Prize location: opposite disco, next to Chinese restaurant, one-way street, heavy traffic
Lge. recep. rm.:   tiny
Col. TV: being repaired, (no room anyway)
2 beds. (1 double):   both small, no room for furniture – double, peeling wallpaper and damp; single, window wouldn't open
Diner: none
Newly-fitted kitchen and b/wc: rusty taps, broken table
Balc.:   not mentioned
Back gdn.:   tiny, not well kept, rubbish
Gge.:   £40 extra per month
Sunny: shaded by house next door and trees
Close tube, buses, shops: too close
Gas c.h.:   could be dangerous

Activity 2
Lamps: cornering
Wipers: rain-sensitive
Cylinders: choice of 2–4
Panels: plastic
Lock: remote control
Steering: 4-wheel
Navigation: computer system
Monitor: computer program – drowsiness
Tyres: twin
Steering: variable, power-assisted
Brakes: anti-lock
Suspension: automatic adjustment

Unit 13
Behind superstitions

Activity 1
True: 3, 5, 6, 9, 10
False: 1, 2, 4, 7, 8

Activity 2
1B;   2D;   3C;   4A;   5C

Unit 14
The language of argument

Activity 1
1D;   2C;   3C;   4A

Activity 2
1–4;   2–7;   3–2;   4–8;   5–1;   6–5;   7–3;   8–6

Unit 15
Points of view

Activity 1
True: 4, 5, 7, 9
False: 1, 2, 3, 6, 8, 10

Activity 2
1B;   2D;   3B;   4C

Unit 16
A roof over your head

Activity 1
Students should have ticked number 1

Activity 2

	Chateau on the Loire	Villa on the Cote d'Azur
period required?	last 2 weeks of August	last 2 weeks of August
no, of bedrooms?	5	4
no, of bathrooms?	2	3
other rooms?	2	2
to sleep max.?	8 – 9	8
swimming - pool?	no	yes
maid service?	—	—
other attractions?	horse - riding	beautiful furnishing, open fire place, near beach, sea views, garden
rental cost per week?	£652	£712

1 Chateau Lafitte
6 House in Sainte Maxime

Unit 17
Inferences

Activity 1
Students should have ticked the following:
1, 3, 4, 5, 8, 9, 11, 12, 13, 14

Activity 2
True: 2, 3, 4, 6
False: 1, 5, 7, 8, 9, 10

Unit 18
Complaints

Activity 1
Students should have ticked the following:
3, 4, 5, 6, 8, 9, 10, 11

Activity 2
1B; 2C; 3D; 4A

Test 1

First part
1 athletics 1; golf 2; cycling 3; horse-racing 4;
cricket 5; showjumping 6; squash 7; karate 8
2C; 3D; 4C

Second part
1 Students should have ticked the following:
1, 2, 3, 5
2C; 3C; 4D

Third part
Reading clockwise, starting by the door:
A, D, G, F, B, C, H, E

Test 2

First part
Students should have ticked the following:
1, 2, 4, 6

Second part
1D; 2C; 3C; 4A; 5B

Third part
1A; 2B; 3D; 4A

Tapescript

Activity I

Section 1

Norman I think she looks a bit smarmy, actually, the woman in that one, a bit scornful, stuck-up, you know the sort. Nose in the air, prim smile.

Bert Yeah, I know the sort. Thinks she's superior to the artist, really, but she can't wait for the portrait to be done so she can see herself up there on the wall in a frame and show the neighbours, eh?

Norman Got a funny face, hasn't she? Those high eyebrows and that long nose . . . heavy eyelids too, quite a strong jaw, a forceful sort of lady. Looks like a schoolmistress.

Bert Yeah, symmetrical sort of face, isn't it? Wonder what she's got her mouth open for. Maybe she's stifling a yawn or something or maybe . . .

Norman Maybe she was going to tell the painter to hurry up and get it over.

Bert Here, come on. Let's go and have a look at that one over there . . .

Section 2

Bert Ah, now there's a face I like. An intellectual face. Serious, thoughtful, nice high forehead . . .

Norman Quite young too. How many years would you give him, Bert?

Bert Difficult to say, really. Late twenties? Early thirties?

Norman Funny, I was going to say less.

Bert But if you look closely he's got wrinkles, hasn't he, and that's not a young man's beard.

Norman Maybe not. I was looking at the wavy hair . . . Funny eyes though. Disturbing eyes. They stare at you. Have you seen the bump on the bridge of the nose?

Bert A really bushy beard, isn't it? I wonder how he managed to kiss his wife.

Section 3

Norman Well, it says 'seated woman', so there must be a seated woman in there somewhere.

Bert I can't see any seated woman, Norm. No seated woman there. Here, wait a minute though . . .

I think I've seen the nose.

Norman Nose? Where? I can see a hand, but it's only got four fingers, I think. Where's that nose you say?

Bert Ah, I've got an eye now, and a mouth, and she's wearing a hat.

Norman Oh, now I'm with it. Got the nose there, and that must be an ear next to it.

Bert No, it is truly a fine piece of modern art but it does require an effort to appreciate it fully . . . and concentration . . . and intelligence.

Norman What? Hey, these knobbly bits at the bottom, what are they? Are they her knees or are they parts of the armchair?

Bert A fine portrait. The painter has tried to get below the surface of the subject.

Norman If a painter painted a portrait of me like that, I'd smash it over his head.

Section 4

Bert I'm not sure I like the look of him much. He looks somehow a bit . . . don't know how to say it . . . *disturbed.*

Norman Very intense, the look. Those eyes really burn a hole in you, don't they?

Bert Yeah, and the high forehead and those high cheekbones . . . They're sort of . . .

Norman I'd like it better if he were looking straight at me. Hey, do you think he was going bald, or did he just have his hair cut short?

Bert Don't know. You'd have to ask him. Looks like an escaped convict to me.

Norman He's got swollen eyes too. He reminds me a bit of E.T., Bert.

Bert Yes, he would, Norm.

Activity 2

Anne Oh, yes, I see. So am I right, Marion, that Chinese horoscopes work on a totally different system from ours?

Marion Oh yes. Instead of the twelve signs we know – Aquarius, Pisces and so on – the Chinese divide people into twelve basic types according to the year they're born in, and then they call each year in the twelve-year cycle by the name of an animal.

Anne And each year, each animal, has different characteristics then?

Marion That's right. Do you want to try it? Try it on yourself, I mean.

Anne	Well, I was born in 1956, so what does that make me?
Marion	1956? Oh, that's a good one! That makes you a Monkey.
Anne	That's what my parents used to call me, but I think they meant something else.
Marion	Actually, it's an interesting sign, the Monkey. Interesting years, Monkey years, too, if you think about it. 1968, 1980, 1956, 1944, years when lots of things seem to happen, often rather confusing things.
Anne	What sort of characteristics do Monkeys have then?
Marion	Well, let me tell you the black side first. It's strange that of all the twelve signs in the Chinese system, the Monkey sign has been used as a sort of 'dustbin-sign', a sign where lots of rather unpleasant characteristics have been thrown together, to stand beside the one great Monkey characteristic, which is intelligence.
Anne	Oh dear. That doesn't sound very encouraging. *Really* unpleasant?
Marion	Get ready for it. Liar, hypocrite, charlatan, pretender, basically unstable . . . and a whole lot more.
Anne	Goodness! I don't know if I want to hear any more.
Marion	But . . . but . . . but . . .
Anne	That's a relief.
Marion	I must say I've always tried to compare the characteristics of each sign with people I know, to see if they fit their animal. In eleven of the animals, the characteristics usually fit to a very large extent, but . . . but the one sign that rarely seemed to fit, if ever, was the Monkey, until, after a long time, I realised why.
Anne	I was beginning to give up hope for the whole Monkey race.
Marion	You see, the trouble is that in Chinese literature they look at the Monkey from the outside . . . they describe him as the world sees him . . . and that's deceptive, misleading. Because then the Monkey gets accused of being a gambler, a manipulator, a conspirator, one who wants to rule others, to decide everything for himself, to have a frightful superiority complex, but . . . but what gets forgotten is, that precisely because of his quality of intelligence the Monkey does tend naturally to dominate intellectually and make wise decisions.
Anne	So the superiority complex is somehow justified?
Marion	In a way, because the Monkey does tend to be the animal best adapted to life in this world, and to get the best out of it. And that provokes envy and misunderstanding.
Anne	What other characteristics do Monkeys have?
Marion	Lots . . . vivacity, fantasy, imagination, a capacity to adapt to circumstances, to change characters, to act the role that circumstances require.
Anne	I suppose that's where the reputation for hypocrisy comes from?
Marion	Yes, although if you look at it from the point of view of your job, say, as an interviewer, it's a positive thing, because it means you can put yourself mentally in the shoes of the people you have to interview, adapt to them, find ways of making them talk.
Anne	Yes, true . . . I see what you mean.
Marion	And then there's a great facility for expression, a hatred for routine, repetition, regularity . . . Monkeys love being given a challenge to motivate and stimulate them, challenges to their ingenuity.
Anne	Maybe that is true in my case. I do get bored very easily.
Marion	On top of that, Monkeys are independent, with a gift for quick reactions. Although they sometimes lack perseverance and concentration . . . as you say, they get bored if they're stuck with one problem for long.
Anne	This really is making me think. I see myself in this, quite clearly.
Marion	Do you spread your interests widely? Monkeys do. They have this great curiosity for things, a real thirst for all sorts of knowledge. And in fact they really know a lot . . . the only trouble is that because they tend to have an open spontaneous attitude, people sometimes take them for superficial, shallow . . .
Anne	That's an occupational hazard of being an interviewer, I think.
Marion	Now one of the Monkey's main troubles comes from this spontaneity, in fact, because people do get put off by it. The Monkey gets the reputation for being a know-all, and people shy away from that and reproach him for it, and reject him. Monkeys usually manage to take that with humour – they've got a good sense of humour and irony and know how to laugh at themselves – but if their humour fails them, they can get very depressed and pessimistic, embittered, sceptical.
Anne	Yes, yes.
Marion	They're generous, they take a lot of interest in others, they like talking to people, but often their intelligence stops them actually feeling how others feel.
Anne	You mean mentally they understand others, but not *emotionally*?
Marion	Yes, that's it. They hear another person's problem and think, 'Gosh, how stupid! Why don't you do this or that and solve it instead of sitting here moaning about it?' Whereas the problem might be requiring more than a quick mental solution. And, tied in with the same thing, people think Monkeys

are insensitive because they don't seem to show feeling, whereas what really happens is that their feelings pass first through the filter of their intelligence, and that often stops their expression.

Anne Well, sorry to break in here, but we must just pause for a break for commercials. We'll be back on the air with more about Chinese horoscopes just one minute from now . . .

Unit 2
Work

Activity I

1 Well, for my job I wear flame-retardant overalls, heavy duty gloves, safety-glasses, and a face shield . . . and . . . a hard hat of course, and steel-toed shoes that are covered by giant, wooden, heat-resistant sandals, and that all tends to disguise the fact that I'm a woman. I earn about £12,000 a year on the job, so I suppose I can afford to wear more feminine gear when I'm not working. When I went to the interview the man offering the job tried his best to put me off, of course, but I stuck out for it and here I am. It's dangerous at times . . . every department has drawbacks, of course, in some it's dust, in others heat, but really the only health threat that worries me, that I do lose a bit of sleep over, is the gas emissions from the coke ovens.

2 It's a routine job, really, but there still aren't many women doing it. I work from 8.30 till about 5.30 or so. In the mornings it's mostly taking stuff to residents, businesses and so on, and in the afternoons I make pick-ups from stores, and then after 5.00, any stuff left over from the mornings. That means there's quite a bit of overtime working. I like the work and it's quite well-paid really. At first I had to go out with an experienced operator, to show me the ropes like, and learn how to deal with the paperwork. Drawbacks? . . . Mother Nature, mainly. Sometimes you get cold and wet, or just plain irritated, like when you have a fall in the mud, or when you drop your biro in a puddle because your fingers are freezing . . .

3 I was a medical technician originally, then I got into a restaurant business, but I was getting nowhere, so when I saw the ad for this job I thought why not and now I've been here six years. It's my job to coordinate all the open-pit operations . . . directly under my supervision I've got three foremen and a crew of twenty truck drivers and eighteen digging equipment-operators. It was rough at first, worse than in other jobs because, well, there's still a deep tradition in this work, especially below ground, a superstition that women bring bad luck. So on my first day I had the doubtful honour of having a petition signed by the men to get me away . . . but they're used to me now, and they've come to respect me . . .

4 I was a licenced beautician, actually, but as a farmer's daughter I'd had experience in manipulating heavy farm equipment . . . still it had never crossed my mind that I'd ever need that experience in a job. The work isn't all that hard . . . I mean, *I* don't have to lift anything heavy – the machine does the hard work. But you do have to be quite strong to work the levers and the noise bothers

me a bit, and the dirt sometimes. I did a two-year
apprenticeship run by the union . . . where they gradually
break you into all sorts of construction machinery.
I chose this particular machine because I was walking
down a street once and I saw one at work on a building
site, and I thought, 'That looks fun, picking things up off
the floor and putting them in the right place' . . .

Activity 2

Phil   Well, with us today we've got Marion Collins of
the *Daily News*. Marion, you've been doing
articles on the problems of women doing blue-
collar jobs – that is, manual and industrial work
haven't you?

Marion   Yes, yes, that's right. The subject's come up partly
because of an American film which features a girl
who works as a welder, and, as I say, partly as
a result of that, the interest among women for
heavy jobs that used to be considered a male
preserve has grown.

Phil   Although in the film, in fact, the girl welder does in
the end become a ballet dancer, doesn't she,
which spoils the effect a bit?

Marion   Yes, you're right, she does, but at least the point's
made – that there is absolutely no reason why a
woman can't do a manual, well, or industrial job,
and still stay recognisably feminine, if that's what
she wants.

Phil   What *are* the problems that women get in blue-
collar jobs?

Marion   Well, I think it all depends on what women
expect. You know if they go into it with their eyes
open, they shouldn't get many problems. But,
anyway, there are a number of things they should
get worked out in their own minds before they
apply. Health's the first. She needn't be a
superwoman, but she should realise that blue-
collar workers are generally healthier and fitter
than average, oh, and that she'll probably be
required to perform strenuous tasks in the job.
She should preferably have a car, because public
transport to and from most manual work places
can be inadequate. And she should also realise
that blue-collar jobs usually work on a seniority
system, which means that if she's a recent arrival,
she'll be among the first to be laid off in any
economic recession.

Phil   I suppose she ought to have some enthusiasm for
the work, too?

Marion   Oh yes, if they think blue-collar jobs aren't
ladylike, they'd better not apply, because it's true
that on-the-job harrassment and off-the-job
prejudice still exist.

Phil   Do men on the job really still resent the presence
of women?

Marion   Well, it's difficult to generalise, because a lot of the
women I've interviewed have said, 'Oh no, the
men we work with are just great.' But there's no
doubt that it can be a problem – resentment – and
it's probably good to go to the job expecting to be
tested . . .

Phil   Expecting the worst, in other words?

Marion   Yes, and that means that women have to expect
to be harrassed and teased . . . but, but women
who become successful in non-traditional jobs
tend to say they handled the daily teasing at first
by not rising to it, and after a while they won the
men's respect. On top of that, too, of course, you
need to talk things over with husbands,
boyfriends, children and friends, if *they* object,
because you do need their understanding and
support.

Phil   Are the hours of work the same in blue-collar
jobs?

Marion   I was just coming to that, actually, because there
can be problems if you have to work on, say, night
shifts or rotating shifts – that's, say, 3.00 to 11.00
one week and 11.00 to 7.00 the next. Blue-collar
jobs often start earlier than white-collar ones, so if
you've got school-age children you may have to
leave home earlier than they do. It's a good idea to
find out all about hours and overtime before you
take on a blue-collar job.

Phil   Aren't . . . a lot of blue-collar jobs normally . . .
dirty? Unpleasant?

Marion   There is truth in that, yes. Any woman wanting a
blue-collar job should be realistic about what she
can stand and what she can't. For example, her
tolerance of heights, of working outside in very
hot or cold weather . . . or of how much heavy
work she can do . . . lifting, shovelling, carrying . . .
because the men won't tolerate passengers on the
job. And noise and smells, can she stand loud noise
or ghastly smells for long? Well she'd have to
sometimes, the smells in a chemical factory or a
paper mill can be dreadful. That's not to say, of
course, that every blue-collar job has these
drawbacks, but many of them . . . they occur in
relatively unpleasant environments.

Phil   What about boredom? There are a lot of boring
jobs, aren't there, among non-traditional jobs? Like
assembly-line working.

Marion   Yes, there's a tremendous range of work amongst
blue-collar jobs . . . anything from, you know, really
interesting things to pushing the same button a
thousand times a day, so it's important to choose
well.

Phil   I suppose you've got to start at the bottom of the
ladder, have you?

Marion   You have, indeed. Whatever industry you go into,
unless you've had some good training or

experience before, you'll probably be at entry level, so you'll be stuck in a not-very-exciting job for a year or so. And you may also be given the worst kind of jobs at first, by the men in charge, as a kind of test of your toughness.

Phil All this sounds terribly hard on the woman. I mean, it sounds as if any woman actually wanting a blue-collar job would have to some sort of firebrand revolutionary.

Marion It is tough, yes, but all you really need is a bit more confidence than average, and the courage to stick things out. You must be confident that you can do the job, knowing what sort of conditions to expect. It's . . . I suppose what you most need is to be realistic.

Unit 3
Decoding information

Activity I

Now on the Philae obelisk, the name Cleopatra is mentioned, and in both of the names Ptolemy and Cleopatra, the letters L and P occur, so if we can identify the letter P, we shall not only have gained a letter but be able to say at which end of the cartouches the names begin. Now, if we write down the names of Ptolemy and Cleopatra as they usually occur in hieroglyphics, we have, in Ptolemy, a series of seven symbols, and in Cleopatra, eleven. We must remember before we start that the Greek form of Ptolemy is Ptolemaios, ending A–I–O–S. Now, on looking at the two names . . . No, let me get you to do the work. Write down the numbers one to seven for Ptolemy across the top of the upper cartouche, and then one to eleven for Cleopatra across the top of the lower one. All right? Then, below those numbers, try to follow my instructions and form the hieroglyphs . . . draw them. Right? Now letter number five in Cleopatra's name is the same as number one in Ptolemy's, in form it's nearly a square. Draw that in then. Now judging by its position only in the names, that letter must represent a P. We also see that letter number two in Cleopatra's name is the same as the fourth in Ptolemy's, the letter that looks like a sphinx in profile looking left, and from their position in the names they must represent the letter L. Now as only one of the names begins with the letter P, the one beginning with that letter is going to be Ptolemy. Now, where are we? Letter number four in Cleopatra's name and letter number three in Ptolemy's are identical, a letter like a hangman's rope, with the noose in the lower left-hand corner, and the rope goes straight up, then curves across to the right and then goes down again to the bottom. Got it? That has the value of some vowel sound like O. Now the letter between P and O in Ptolemy must be a T, which is the same as letter number ten in Cleopatra, so we can fill that one in, the T . . . it looks like the tip of the rising or setting sun. Right? Next fill in the last letter of Ptolemy's name, the S. That's an easy one . . . it looks a bit like an S in the top half but the lower half is straightened out, so it looks like a walking stick with a long, curved handle. Now letters six and nine in Cleopatra's name, which correspond to an A. What you need for your As is a symbol that looks like an eagle in profile, an eagle standing and facing left. Draw that in then, for letters six and nine. Now, there is a symbol that looks like an old-fashioned razor standing on its handle with its blade on the left, which appears at number three in Cleopatra and, doubled, at number six in Ptolemy. That represents some sort of vowel sound like E, and the double symbol represents the vowel sound of the 'ai' in Ptolemaios. That leaves us only the three peculiar signs at number five in Ptolemy, numbers eight and eleven in Cleopatra . . . oh yes, and numbers one and seven in Cleopatra, I was forgetting those, wasn't I? Now in his studies, Young proved that the rising sun symbol always occurred in the names of goddesses, and that when it was united with the symbol that looks like a rolling stone, with the stone below it, this marked a feminine termination of a name, pronounced '-tra', so add your rolling stone at number eleven in Cleopatra's name. Now by elimination we know that number five in Ptolemy must be an M, and number eight in Cleopatra must be an R. The M looks like a long letter U, but turned on its side with its open end on the right, all right? And the number eight in Cleopatra . . . that looks like a flattened disc, a bit like a flying saucer. Now, what does that leave us? Ah yes, the first letter in Cleopatra, which is a right-angled triangle with the vertical line on the right. And the number seven in Cleopatra . . . the number seven, that's like a left hand, a left hand chopped off at the wrist, and seen from the side, but with the thumb on top. Right? Now we're complete then, at least, I hope we are. Well, I wish you good luck with the task . . .

Activity 2

Tim Well today we've been in radio contact with the British Himalayan expedition. We're going to play you a recording of Wally's latest message, which was picked up by our correspondent in Kathmandu about half an hour ago. The reception on the message is pretty awful in parts, but remember Wally's stuck up there with the team at about 22,500 feet in the middle of a blizzard. We think you'll be interested to hear Wally, anyway, and you can probably follow what he's talking about, if you refer to the map on the screen.

Wally Hello, hello, Wally Turnbull here from base camp at 22,500 feet. We set up the radio transmitter here back on Saturday, in the good weather . . . can you hear me?

Voice Yes, yes. Go on, go on.

Wally Hello . . . right . . . and then on Sunday we made quite good progress and managed to establish a small advance camp at about 24,500 feet on Sunday morning. That's a camp on the shoulder of land just at the bottom of the slope up to Mount Satyavan. Then on Sunday afternoon we tried to consolidate our position up there at the advance camp, but things started to go wrong and it turned out much

more difficult than it need have done. First, not far from base camp, and in perfect visibility, one of the porters had a fall on the ice . . . he wasn't hurt, but he *was* carrying a load of food supplies, and the whole load fell down a deep crevasse in the ice. On top of that, the other porters got worried by the fall, and it took us a long time to persuade them to go on. Then, when they turned the corner there to start the march up the glacier towards the icefield and . . . the advance camp, they were met with a gale of a wind – the sort of wind you simply can't take risks with – so that slowed them down a lot. Then a bit higher up the glacier, as if the wind wasn't enough, about halfway up the glacier, halfway to the advance camp that is, there was an avalanche falling from Mount Savitri onto the glacier, which made things dangerous and blocked the way . . . so more time was wasted as they dug themselves out of that. Anyway, the advance camp wasn't consolidated till about 4.00 on Sunday afternoon. And from there it was hoped to make an assault on Mount Satyavan on Monday morning. But that had to be postponed indefinitely because of the weather. Later on Monday the blizzard slackened a bit, and Tom Brown and Frank Bannerman began the climb up to try to establish a camp for themselves as near to the summit as they could. In fact they wanted to set up a camp on the ridge at about 26,700 feet, to be able to make a final assault on the summit yesterday, but they were slowed down severely by the wind, and in the end they had to strike camp halfway to the ridge, at about 25,900 feet. And on the way they had two shocks. Lower down, near the bottom of the slope, they both heard a very strange noise, and I must admit they did think just for a moment that it could be an abominable snowman, a yeti or whatever you call it, though they didn't see anything much for the snow. And then, a bit higher up, Frank had a fall that could have been very nasty indeed . . . in fact he came to rest right on the edge of a precipice but the rope saved him going down. Close thing though. And now, as you know, we're stuck here, the weather's turned awful, it's really nasty. I'll be back in touch this afternoon if there are any developments . . .

Unit 4
Processes and procedures

Activity 1

Irene Well, it's time now for our 'Dish of the Day' spot, and here's our resident – what shall we call you, Vincent? – gastronomic adviser? . . . cordon bleu, Vincent Jung. What's on the menu today, Vincent?

Vincent Whew . . . excuse my being slightly out of breath dear listeners, but the studio lift decided to play one of its tricks between the floor below and this one . . . yes, well, today's dish is *coq au vin*, which for those of you who have forgotten the little French you learned at school is chicken or capon cooked in wine. It just sounds more elegant if it's cooked in French. Right, got your notebooks ready? Here we go. Now, for the delights of *coq au vin* you need about 40 minutes' preparation time and another two hours or so for the cooking. As for the ingredients, well – this is to feed four people, by the way – first you'll need a chicken or a capon . . . you won't get far without one of those . . . preferably not one of those horrible, plastic, tasteless chickens they sell in supermarkets, but if there's nothing better I suppose you'll have to make do with that . . . a chicken of about 1½ kilos . . . then you need *bouquet garni* – we're all French today – that's one of those little bags of mixed herbs for flavouring . . . salt, black pepper, about 100 grams of streaky bacon, 100 grams of small onions, one large clove of garlic, 100 grams of button mushrooms, 50 grams of unsalted butter, one tablespoon of olive oil, two tablespoons of brandy, half a litre of red wine – any drinkable red wine will do, so don't go overboard – a quarter of a litre of stock, and mix some *beurre manié* (yet more French – that's that mixture of butter and flour you use for thickening sauces). Then garnish with 100 grams of lightly fried onions, 50 grams of button mushrooms, and level tablespoonful of chopped parsley.

Irene That's it for the ingredients, is it, Vincent?

Vincent Indeed it is. Now for the good bit. Here's how to cook the bird. Approach it, as one Japanese refrigerator instruction manual once said, as if it were your friend. First clean it and tie it up. Right? Use the giblets with the *bouquet garni* of herbs, a bit of salt and some freshly ground pepper to make stock. Then chop up the bacon, peel the onions and garlic and trim and slice the mushrooms. OK? . . . Next heat the butter and oil in a casserole, and fry the bacon in it till the fat runs . . . then remove it from the casserole and brown the bird all over in the hot fat, spooning off any surplus fat afterwards. Right? Next, warm the brandy in a spoon or small pan, set it alight, and pour it while it's still flaming over the bird. As soon as the flames die down – and don't set fire to your kitchen, will you – pour in the wine and add the bacon, onions, mushrooms and crushed garlic. Pour over enough stock to make the liquid come halfway up the bird. Then cover with a lid and cook over low heat on top of the stove or in the oven at 150°C – that's gas mark 2, not hot in other words – for at least a couple of hours or till the bird is tender, turning it from time to time. Next, remove the bird and divide it into joints, keeping them warm on a serving dish. Lift out the onions, bacon and mushrooms with a perforated spoon, and arrange them over the chicken. Reduce the cooking liquid by brisk boiling, then lower the heat and gradually beat in pieces of the *beurre manié* until the sauce has thickened. Correct the seasoning and pour the sauce over the chicken. Finally, serve, garnished, with small glazed onions, fried or grilled button mushrooms, and freshly chopped parsley. Well, that's the dish for the day, dear dishy listeners, and I hope you and your families or guests enjoy it . . .

Activity 2

Jane Well, Ian Duncan, who's with us today, is the sound engineer with number-one, chart-topping rock group 'Fireball'. Ian, just to get things clear from the start, could you begin by telling us exactly what the responsibilities of a sound engineer are.

Ian Yes . . . I'd say basically he's the person you see in rock concerts who's out there in the audience on a platform with a mixing table . . .

Jane A mixing table's one of those tables with lots of control levers and sound-level indicators, isn't it?

Ian That's right, like the one you've got in the control room here in the studio, actually, more or less.

Jane And it's your job to make sure the sounds of the instruments on the stage are correctly balanced, isn't it?

Ian Yes, yes. So that the singer's voice can be heard clearly, so the guitars are not too loud, so the drums don't drown everything . . .

Jane And you do this acoustically . . . or electronically?

Ian A bit of both, actually. The mixer, the machine, works electronically, of course . . . which means that the sounds of all the separate instruments on the stage are fed directly into the mixing system – each one having its own channel – and then the level of sound on each channel can be watched on the channel indicator . . . that's a sort of gauge, you know, like the ones you see on good tape recorders . . . and if the sound engineer sees from his indicators that a particular instrument is louder, is coming through louder than the others, or is too soft, too low, he can use his channel controls . . . they're called potentiometers, in fact, they're power levers . . . to adjust the volume, up or down. Now the engineer works with headphones on, of course, but at the same time one of his assistants will be listening acoustically, er, that is, without headphones . . .

Jane As if he were one of the audience . . .?

Ian That's it. To keep an acoustic check so that the mixture the audience is hearing is the best possible.

Jane This is probably a dumb question, actually, but . . . can't the musicians tell for themselves whether the sound is good or not?

Ian That's what a lot of people ask, naturally . . . are engineers really necessary? Well, the answer is yes, I'm happy to say, and for two main reasons, one technical and the other human. Er, you see, technically speaking, first . . . you have to remember that all the public places where rock groups perform have very different acoustic properties . . . I'm sure you'll have heard the old joke about the Royal Albert Hall in London, for example, where the echo . . . the echo is so strong that people say you hear two concerts for the price of one . . . So of course, to fill a large public place, a cinema say, with sound, especially when the place is packed with people, because human bodies absorb sound, all that requires high-powered amplifiers and speakers, which must be arranged in such a way that the sound can reach every corner of the place with as equal a quality as possible. And all that takes many hours of work and needs an expert to do it . . .

Jane And I suppose the musicians are somehow too much in the middle of the sound to know.

Ian Oh yes, they've got no idea of what they sound like at the back. The other thing is that the drummer, say, may not even be able to hear what the musician next to him's playing . . .

Jane So what you do in a way is to act as a kind of representative of the audience, but with the power to adjust things technically when things go wrong . . . But what about the human reason you mentioned?

Ian Yes, well, that's quite amusing sometimes. As an engineer I'm a fairly objective, scientific sort of person, and I can't help feeling that one good reason for having an engineer is that there's a natural tendency for the instruments in the front line to want to outshout each other. I mean, if you leave them to look after themselves what usually happens is that, say, a guitarist has to play a solo, so he turns up his volume, then forgets to turn it down . . .

Jane And the others turn theirs up to match him?

Ian Yes, and the whole thing gets out of hand till no one can hear a blind thing of what's going on. And the spiral normally ends in an argument.

Jane So you act as a kind of referee for them.

Ian That's it. They grumble at me, often, but deep down they know it's for their own good.

Jane One last thing, Ian. What advice would you give to young groups that are starting out and having to play in places with bad acoustics, who can't afford a sound engineer?

Ian Yes, I know how they feel very well. You go to some place where the stage is cramped, and the mains socket's broken, and so on. Well, what I would say is: Don't despair, and try to learn how to evaluate the acoustics of the places you play in. A simple handclap will tell you a lot about the acoustics of a room, you know. If it's a long room with a low ceiling, for example, you'll find that your bass sound will be swallowed up . . . and of course, the other common hazard is having lots of absorbent surfaces – carpets, people, plants, curtains, furniture – which deaden the sound. Two things you can do. One is to realise it's not perfect and play your real best in defiance of the acoustics. And the other is get a friend of yours who knows the band sound well to move round the room while you're playing and keep you informed of what it's sounding like in . . .

Unit 5
News slant

Activity 1

More than 21 hours after yesterday's occupation of the British Embassy in Semenath, Ruritania, by an armed dissident group calling itself the Ruritanian Liberation Front, the building is still surrounded by the Ruritanian army. Food and drink have been sent into the embassy, and negotiations have been continued intermittently throughout the night by telephone. The Liberation Front have now made their demands clear. In protest, they say in their communiqué, against constant and brutal persecution by the Ruritanian secret police, they want to be escorted to a British Airways plane in Semenath airport and be taken to the neighbouring state of Sylvania, where they have been offered political asylum by President Katro Bendy, a declared opponent of the Ruritanian military dictatorship let by General Augus Loczau, which seized power in a bloody *coup d'état* two years ago. The Front have threatened that if their demands are not carried out by midday today, they will kill one hostage every hour. It is known that at the time of the occupation, there were 45 embassy staff inside the embassy, and, according to Ruritanian police estimates, there may be up to 70 more people trapped in the building. The ambassador and the Liberation Front have been in regular radio contact with the Foreign Office in London, but so far the Foreign Office has refused to issue any statement . . .

Activity 2

Sally   Well, the time's now coming up to twenty-two minutes to eight on this rather grey, grim November morning, or 07.38 if you're the digital kind, and today's first topic for comment is that occupation of the British Embassy in Semenath, Ruritania, by the Ruritanian Liberation Front. To quote a couple of splash headlines from this morning's papers . . . one here in the *Sun* says 'Give the rebels what they want, Loczau', and another one, this time from the *Star* and far more aggressive 'Get 'em out, Loczau, or else . . .' But these things are never simple, of course, because there's the risk to the hostages in the British Embassy and the question of diplomatic immunity, political asylum and so on. Where do things stand legally in fact? Well, let's take some legal advice, and with us we've got Francis Trimble, who's an international lawyer who knows about this . . . these things. And the first question we want to ask you, Francis . . . can't we send in commandos, the SAS or the SBS or some special squad? After all, there were those two famous hijacks in the past,

weren't there, the one at Entebbe Airport in Uganda and the other in the Sudan, and in those cases special forces were sent in, weren't they, by the Israelis and the Germans. And of course there was the trouble in the Iranian Embassy here in London a couple of years ago, when our SAS went in didn't they?

Francis   Oh yes, but they were very different cases, you know. You cannot legally compare, in legal terms I mean, a hijack with what has happened out there in Ruritania. And in the case of the Iranian Embassy in London, which at first sight seems to have similarities, because of the fact that an embassy building was involved, you have to remember that it was a group of Arab–Iranian dissidents who occupied the building in protest against the Khomeini regime, and that it was the Khomeini government which asked the British government to send our troops in.

Sally   I see . . . and in this case the exact parallel would have been if the group occupying our embassy in Ruritania had been a group of British dissidents protesting against the British government?

Francis   That's the parallel with the Iranian Embassy case here in 1981, and the parallel with the case in Ruritania now would be if a group of British dissidents had occupied say the Ruritanian Embassy in London and demanded to be flown from Heathrow to France.

Sally   And I suppose it's highly unlikely that the Ruritanian government of General Loczau is going to ask the British army for help with its own dissidents?

Francis   I would say it is extremely unlikely, yes.

Sally   In legal terms, what stops General Loczau from sending in his troops to storm the building? Is that to do with diplomatic immunity?

Francis   It is, yes. The British Embassy, any embassy on any foreign territory, is regarded in law as the sovereign territory of the state holding it, not of the host country.

Sally   So the British Embassy in Semenath is considered as British soil?

Francis   That's correct, yes. And the Ruritanians would only go in if the ambassador or our Government asked them to.

Sally   Which they won't do.

Francis   No, it would be very risky. Both the Ruritanian army and the Liberation Front have a pretty bloodthirsty reputation, and if our Government asked the Loczau regime to send in troops there would undoubtedly be a bloodbath. That's not a legal opinion, it's my own.

Sally   So in this case the diplomatic immunity works in our favour, protecting our Embassy people?

Francis   Indeed it does. This is precisely the sort of case protected under the terms of the Vienna Convention of 1961.

Sally But what about the journey from the embassy to the airport, supposing the Loczau regime accedes to the demands of the Liberation Front?

Francis Well, there you're out of the realm of law and into practical politics. There's no question of diplomatic immunity there, of course, but you can be quite sure that the Liberation Front will take an important hostage with them, or two or three, probably the ambassador for one of them, and it would be political dynamite if, having given its undertaking not to fire, General Loczau's troops broke the agreement and any of our diplomats were killed. But again I stress that that is a private, not a legal, opinion.

Sally Well, thank you very much, Francis Trimble, for joining us so early on this drizzly winter morning.

Francis Not at all. I only hope that . . .

Activity 3

Sally Well, how about having a politician's view of the Ruritanian affair, the occupation of the British Embassy in Semenath, Ruritania, by the Ruritanian Liberation Front. We've got a politician on the line now, actually not on the line as he's up there in our Sheffield studios, none other than Frank Butterworth, Opposition spokesman on Foreign Affairs and MP for Barnsley East. Good morning, Mr Butterworth.

Frank Morning.

Sally Is there any advice you can give the Government in this situation, or do you think they're handling it as best they can at the present moment?

Frank Well, the Foreign Office hasn't said much yet, has it, to say the least, but as far as I can tell I think they're handling it pretty well so far. The obligation of course in cases like this is to stay cool and not do those things which our hearts prompt rather than our heads. I mean above all that we should at all times remember that there are 45 British Embassy staff stuck in that building, most of them British nationals, and quite apart from them there are nine or ten thousand British nationals working in Ruritania, mostly on aid projects. And don't let's forget either that in General Loczau's two years in power, his army and secret police have proved pretty effective, pretty good at, I think they call it, 'controlling' the Opposition to the regime, which normally means making them disappear off the map, and they've been rather violent about it. And the Liberation Front too, they're no slouches either, are they, they've been pretty good at blowing up people and so on, so I feel strongly that it's in our own interests to play it cool and keep the negotiations going. Keep talking, that's what I always say.

Sally Recently you've been on record as saying you think Britain should break off diplomatic relations with the Loczau regime. Do you stand by that now?

Frank Oh I do, I do indeed. The Loczau regime is a military dictatorship with no popular support, and I think they've proved in the last two years that they've got as much idea about governing a country as my dog – less, probably – and in no way could they be said to have the national interests of Ruritania at heart, or to represent them. And if I were the British Government, I would have no truck with them at all, in fact I think we were too ready to recognise them in the first place. No, I think we should decide here and now that when this crisis . . . incident . . . is past, as we hope it will be very soon, we should have a very careful look at our relations with that regime, and yes, if I were Minister, I would take the necessary steps to break off relations.

Sally But there are something like 10,000 British nationals in Ruritania, aren't there, mostly working on aid projects. Would you simply abandon those aid projects? After all, Ruritania's a very poor country, isn't it, and if we broke off relations, I suppose the people we would harm most would be precisely those Ruritanians who are getting the most benefit from our presence . . . the poor, I mean.

Frank It's a complicated question, that, I agree, and of course we have to be careful that we don't do harm to the poor and needy in Ruritania, but equally I feel that Loczau's military regime has only survived these two years because it's had support from nations like ourselves, and I feel if we behaved with principle, with integrity, and broke off relations, to put pressure on the regime, and if we could persuade some other nations, like France or the Germans, to follow suit, I think the regime would topple, just collapse, overnight.

Sally The trouble is though, isn't it, that the Liberation Front also has a pretty ugly reputation for rather indiscriminate guerrilla violence, hasn't it? I mean, if we support them, won't we be going from the frying pan into the fire a bit?

Frank Well, this is a typical Third World situation, isn't it . . . I mean, a military oligarchy backed up by a very rich minority and foreign powers using strong-arm terror methods to maintain themselves in power, and so what can the Opposition do in a case like that but go underground and fight a guerrilla war . . . violence breeds violence . . .

Sally So you think the Liberation Front's violence is justified, even if innocent parties get killed?

Frank Hang on there a minute . . . I'd say, not so much that it is justifiable as that it is entirely understandable, but in saying that, may I make it quite clear that I earnestly hope that they have the political sense not to kill any of those hostages they've got in the British Embassy, and that General Loczau, for once in his life, behaves like a statesman and allows them to get out of the country. And I feel that if we keep cool and keep them talking, there will be a . . . satisfactory ending.

Sally Mr Butterworth, thank you very much.

Frank Not at all. Thank you.

Unit 6
Schedules

Activity I

Well, today, if you're footloose and fancy free and you want to be out in the open air in this beautiful August weather, have you thought of spending the day at Burnwell's Three-Day Agricultural Show, the biggest event of its kind in the country? It's all happening there all right – today's the second day, and . . . let's see what they've got on there today. Well, there's county cricket, Derbyshire against Yorkshire, play starting at 11.30 and finishing at 6.30 on the Recreation Ground, with a special temporary car park south of the ground . . . Then for rock fans there's six hours of it starting at around six this evening in the special rock festival precinct, with several local groups including Memphis from Manchester, but the main attraction comes around about ten with a concert by the Police – that's not the real police because they'll be dealing with the crowds and traffic, we hope – but the *the* Police, the real famous ones. There are some tickets still available and some won't be put on sale till after lunch, at the box office in the precinct. For the kiddies, and let's face it, for the grown-ups too, the fair will be open till about two in the morning, and if you get bored there's always Haddon Castle, which'll be open to the public from ten till eight, with its miniature railway, go-karts, mini-zoo, etcetera, plus all the attractions of the castle itself. The entry gate's on the London Road just south of the town. Right, what else? As for the show itself, well, in the morning in the Main Ring, number one, there'll be all the demonstrations of agricultural machinery, and in the afternoon a sheepdog demonstration (with real dogs and real sheep I should add) . . . that's starting at two o'clock after lunch and it'll go on for two and a half hours or so, till the sheep get fed up with being pushed around, I suppose. Then at five or thereabouts there'll be a parade of prize-winning animals, if that's your cup of tea. In Ring Two, there's going to be show-jumping all morning, with the Derbyshire Junior Cup at ten o'clock for young riders, under-18s, and then the Burnwell Cup Knock-Out starting at about 12.15. In the afternoon there'll be the BSJA international competition, with a lot of top international riders taking part, starting around about 2.45. And, and . . . at two o'clock, and again at five or so, straight after the BSJA competition, there'll be a motorcycle acrobatics display by the Royal Signals Motorcycle team. And they're great. I think that's all as far as the attractions go. Couple of messages from the police – that's the real police, not the musicians – who were tearing their hair out yesterday, when there were apparently 55,000 people at the show . . . it's the good weather that brings them out! The police appeal to drivers to be sensible and patient, and follow their guidelines. Apparently there was a father and mother of a traffic jam in the town centre yesterday so this is in motorists' interests . . . please, the police say, if you're coming from Manchester, use the A15, the A15, *not* the A24, and park near Burnwell station. If you're coming from Birmingham on either the A719 or the A784, you're recommended to follow the signposts up Paternoster Road, past the church to the same station car park. And if you're coming up from Derby or the south, police say you're more likely to find a space in the station car park than you are in the one by the cricket ground. From Nottingham, you've got your car park there on the Ripley Road, and if you're coming from Sheffield, as about ten million people did yesterday, police advise you to go in on the A805, which is a better road, and park in either of the two car parks as you approach Burnwell on the Sheffield Road. And, of course . . .

Activity 2

Well, ladies and gentlemen, I'm very happy to welcome you, on behalf of Visionrama Ltd, to the first weekend seminar on Video Production, and we really do hope you'll get a lot out of this . . . experience. We on this side of the fence get a lot out of this sort of . . . encounter, and we do sincerely hope the benefit will be . . . mutual. Perhaps, perhaps I should introduce myself first . . . my name's Alan Drinkall, and I am the admin. officer on this course, so if you have . . . complaints or suggestions please don't hesitate to . . . propel them in my direction, as it were, and I'll do my best either to solve the problem or in some way try to persuade you that it doesn't exist.

Now . . . before I introduce you to Gillian Allen, the seminar leader, who'll be giving the introductory talk, there are just a few things, admin. things to say, particularly about the timetable. There was a piece of paper face down on your chairs with the name Seminar Programme on it, but you don't need me to tell you that it's only an outline programme, so let's fill in the details in a couple of minutes now.

Now you'll notice that there are on your programme only two groups, marked 'Scripting, etc.' and 'Technical'. Now what has rather caught us by surprise is that there were twelve applicants who expressed a real interest in learning the skills of video acting, that is, of actually being on camera, so we've formed a third group, called 'Acting' for want of a better word . . . So maybe you could add that into your third column, 'Acting, Group 3'. OK, now, let me just

say what the Acting group will be doing and then we'll be able to fill in the additions to the other columns. As you'll see, today the three groups will be working almost entirely independently, but tomorrow, when the purpose will be to prepare and film a short production scripted by the Scripting group, there'll be the chance for the groups to work together so that the final result, we hope, will really be a 100% communal effort.

So just briefly, Acting group, after coffee this morning, 11.15–12.45, Pam Taylor will be putting you through it with some Drama Exercises, Mime and Movement, and so on, to get you warmed up. After lunch, you'll be having a session with the title 'On Camera', which is basically about styles and problems – Pam will be asking you to analyse some TV styles. Then after tea, from 4.00 till 6.00, there'll be a workshop session, called 'On Camera Exercises', where you'll have the chance to get used to seeing yourselves on camera in various exercises. All these sessions will be led by Pam Taylor, by the way.

Ah, yes, tomorrow morning, from 9.15 till 10.45, the Technical group will be having a practical workshop to look at the sort of technical problems that come up in filming, and then the Acting group will be the guinea pigs, OK? After coffee tomorrow, from 11.15 to 12.45 . . . ah, now by then the Scripting group will be ready with their script and that will form the basis of the briefing session for both the Technical group and the actors. Incidentally, both Technical and Acting groups will be encouraged to participate actively in the briefing, giving suggestions and so on. Then of course there'll be the actual filming between 2.00 and 3.30, and the editing and mixing between 4.00 and 6.30 . . . and the actual showing of the film, the masterpiece, and the discussion session, after dinner.

Now just one or two other admin. changes, if I can beg for your patience for a second longer. We've only got one wide-screen TV monitor, and we'd like the Acting group to have the use of that for their 'On Camera' session at 2.00 this afternoon and to make that possible, Ned Grigson has kindly agreed to simply swap round his first two sessions with the Technical group, giving the vision one first and the one on sound second, so group two will be working on sound from 2.00 till 3.30 this afternoon . . . right, sorry to have droned on for so long . . . let me now pass you over to our course leader, Gill Allen, who'll fill you in on many more . . .

Unit 7
Travel

Activity 1

Gail   Today's guest is Mr Stuart Moore, Information ·Officer from London's Heathrow Airport. Welcome to the programme, Mr Moore.

Stuart   Thank you.

Gail   A busy time for you, I suppose, the summer?

Stuart   Well, yes, but things never really let up at Heathrow, you know.

Gail   It used to be called the busiest airport in the world, didn't it?

Stuart   Well, some people still think it is, actually, but it isn't . . . we're in fact fourth in the world. Chicago's O'Hare airport is way out in front with nearly 45 million passengers handled last year. Then comes Atlanta Georgia with 40 million and Los Angeles with 33. Where we do come out in front is with international passengers. Last year we had $27\frac{1}{2}$ million passengers in all, and of those nearly $23\frac{1}{2}$ million were international, and that compares with New York's JFK with about 13, and Frankfurt with 12.

Gail   Which means that a very high proportion of passengers using Heathrow are international.

Stuart   Oh, yes indeed. 85%, compared with only 48% for JFK and 70 for Frankfurt.

Gail   There's one question everybody asks, and that's about the relationship, the distance between Heathrow and the second London airport at Gatwick. A lot of people complain about the distance from . . . well, the distance between the two because of the time and trouble it takes to make a transfer.

Stuart   Yes, the distance is something of a problem, because most people, most air travellers, are accustomed to transferring flights in the same airport, but the problem is precisely that there are so many international flights coming through London and there is no way in which all of them can be accommodated in one airport. Actually, for passengers who are really in a hurry there's a heliport, a helicopter service between the two airports, you know . . . a 15-minute flight for £21, which isn't expensive – it would cost about £40 in a taxi and take you five times longer.

Gail   How about transport into central London from Heathrow?

Stuart   Well, again, it depends on how much you're prepared to spend. A taxi'll cost you about £13 or £14 at the moment and takes about an hour, whereas the Underground link takes about 50 minutes and costs only £1.09p.

Gail   And the tube runs all day long, does it?

Stuart   The tube? No. It runs from five in the morning till just before midnight, but that covers the vast majority of the flights. But you can always get a taxi during the night.

Gail   One thing I've always wondered . . . I mean, there you are with so many international passengers and I suppose many of them are on intercontinental flights . . .

Stuart   Indeed yes.

Gail   The question is nothing to do with Heathrow specifically, actually, but about jet lag. Does your medical department have to deal with lots of cases of jet lag with so many intercontinental people . . .?

Stuart   Oh, indeed, we do yes. I suppose the listeners are . . . will know what jet lag is, will they?

Gail   I'm not sure I'm all that clear myself really . . . it's basically to do with crossing time zones, isn't it?

Stuart   That's right. Very briefly . . . since I think it was 1884, which is somewhat before I was born anyway . . . the world has been divided into 24 time zones, each of 15 degrees of latitude, plus an international date line, with the zero degree line passing through Greenwich, as you know. So for example, the time difference, the time lag, between say New Zealand and Greenwich is twelve hours, and the lag between Greenwich and, say, Cuba is five hours . . .

Gail   Which is like saying Cuba starts its day 17 hours after New Zealand.

Stuart   Now if you cross a large number of time zones in a flight the chances are that you'll suffer some disorientation when you arrive at your destination, because the journey will have disturbed the . . . your hidden body clock that regulates your daily body habits.

Gail   That's called the Circadian rhythm, isn't it?

Stuart   Right, yes, the Circadian or Diurnal rhythms. All the body's activities, waking, sleeping, eating . . . temperature, evaporative water loss, emptying the bowels and so on . . . all that's regulated by the body clock, so if you land after a long flight your body has to cope with trying to conform to the new local time and rhythm of life while all its instincts are . . . to carry on at the same time and rhythm as back home.

Gail   And is there any way of avoiding jet lag?

Stuart   Well, there are a number of things you can do to help yourself. One thing is that you should ask for a hotel room that's as quiet as possible when you arrive, not above a noisy street or near a hotel lift or something. Then on your journey, you should avoid the excesses of airline hospitality . . . on the journey.

Gail   In other words don't eat or drink too much.

19

Stuart That's it. And another thing is to take as much exercise as you can while the seat belt signs are off. And finally there's the question of timing, of timing your arrival to coincide with the normal body bedtime if you can, and if possible take things easy for the first twenty-four hours . . .

Gail There are no drugs you can take then?

Stuart No, at least I don't know of any, except maybe a mild sedative to help you sleep, or a mild laxative to aid . . . digestion . . .

Activity 2

Cairo's contact with Europe was through Venice: in fact these two cities became inseparable in the 14th and 15th centuries because they organised a world monopoly on East–West trade, and historians have even described Venice as a half-oriental city. After the Fourth Crusade, when the Venetians stripped Constantinople and ruled the Levant, and controlled even the Black Sea, the merchants of Venice briefly had had a direct link of their own with the East through their own Levantine ports. But when they lost these ports in 1291 to the Egyptians, the Venetians scandalised the Christian world by making a commercial treaty with the Mamelukes in Cairo which gave them trading rights of a new kind. Venetian merchants and agents now appeared in large numbers in cities like Cairo, and by 1400 Venice was the recognised European mart for exchange of goods from East to West.

Almost everything from the East reaching Venice and the West had to pass through Cairo first, and the customs dues paid on this trade were the real bonanza for Cairo's merchants and Mamelukes and sultans. It was Ibn Said in 1246 who saw and described how goods arriving in Cairo from the Red Sea were bonded in Fustat (the Cairo port) and then distributed to the markets or sent on. D.A. Cameron, in his book *Egypt in the Nineteenth Century* shows how the Mamelukes levied customs dues on every bale of Oriental produce which arrived from the Persian Gulf and the Red Sea for transfer to the harbours of Alexandria and Alexandretta for retransshipment to Venice. Cameron gives us a typical example of a consignment of raw silks, nutmegs, peppers, indigo and cloves. The cargo was worth the equivalent of 22,000 U.S. dollars on landing in Egypt at a Red Sea port where first customs dues were almost $9,000. The goods were then sold at $44,000, and by the time they reached Bulaq in Cairo the price was $66,000. But another $10,000 had to be paid before they could finally be cleared for transshipment to Venice. Thus, whether in customs or in tolls or in presents to the local governors and escorts, a quarter of the $76,000 paid by the Venetian would go to the Mameluke sultan and aristocracy merely for the privilege of transit. Arrived at Venice, the produce might fetch any price from $100,000 to $200,000. The excessive wealth and exotic business that all this trading tribute brought to Cairo convinced Stanley Lane Poole that it was Cairo and not Baghdad that was really the fabulous city of the *Arabian Nights* . . .

Unit 8
Women in society

Activity I

I'm glad that the Ayatollah Khomeini has drawn attention to the situation of women in banks, by creating a fuss over the kind of clothes that women must wear in London-based Iranian banks (very modest clothes, preferably with the head covered). And of course we are all outraged that this medieval-style Middle-Eastern tyrant could be so sexist. Fancy discriminating against women in this way! But let's cut the humbug and get to the root of things: British banks discriminate against women every day of the week. And the sort of sexism practised by the Big Four clearing banks in this country is of a much more invidious kind than mere top-dressing. British banks treat women as a lesser species on the levels of education, opportunity and promotion. Recently I came across a case of two 16-year-old school-leavers who applied to a major bank for jobs. The boy was told that the bank preferred young men to apply when they had acquired some sort of A levels. The girl was told she would have a good chance of a job if she came back after acquiring some O levels. Males are seen as management material; females are viewed as clerical fodder. Small wonder that the vast majority of women working in British banks are indeed concentrated in the lowest clerical grades, and that you scarcely ever meet a senior woman bank official. From recruitment onwards, banks treat women and men differently. And small wonder, either, that so many young women in banking respond by seeing the job as something on a par with the supermarket check-out desk. Changing a cheque at a bank the other day, I noticed that the two young women at the cash counter had got the old Woolworth's store-girl technique down to a fine art: chatting to one another about their private lives while attending with casual competence to the customer. 'Well, I don't know, Sharon, you've been married longer than I have. I mean, I said to him . . .'. I thought: this bank spends millions on advertising and it can't spend tuppence halfpenny on management training . . . There are far more important issues for women's careers at stake than the matter of clothes. Most of us would be willing to dress in cap and bells if the post of court jester carried good prospects, remuneration, and opportunities for advancement.

Activity 2

Pat With us now we've got television director Bill Clanton, who's here to promote his film *Tessa*. And from what I hear, Bill you've just finished a new TV series. What's it about, or must that be kept a secret?

Bill Oh no – it's about friendship, in fact, friendship and feminism.

Pat Why did you choose friendship as a theme?

Bill Well, what I've tried to do in the series is to show four main stages in friendship, kind of like four seasons, and to investigate what happens in those stages.

Pat I suppose the first one is spring?

Bill That is right, yes. The time when everything is new and the whole thing sails along just perfectly.

Pat Which is followed by summer?

Bill When the strong sunlight, how shall I say? . . . searches out all the details, some good, some not so good of the friend . . . it's somehow more realistic than spring.

Pat And summer leads to autumn . . .?

Bill Right, which is when things turn a bit cooler, when you begin to go off people.

Pat When you lose that certainty you had in spring and wonder if it's all been a terrible mistake?

Bill That's it. The cold autumn winds start to blow in the friendship, and then comes winter . . .

Pat Which I suppose is when you are faced with the decision of either accepting the person as he or she really is, with all the defects and annoying habits . . . Sort of agreeing to differ?

Bill Exactly, or of breaking off and breaking new ground.

Pat And how have you dealt with this theme in your series?

Bill I've done it through four couples. They meet first through their wives and then the wives bring the husbands into the circle. The men have this . . . competitive relationship, sort of, like a rivalry, which I think is typical of a lot of men's relationships. It's an insecurity thing, basically . . .

Pat Do you think the Feminist Movement is making it easy for men and women to have a friendship, a non-sexual relationship?

Bill Well, I think they have raised the question, which is helpful. I think we should somehow try to make people see that if a man and woman share an experience in life, or an interest, or share feelings about something, it doesn't necessarily lead to an . . . an emotional entanglement.

Pat When do you think people begin to realise that? I mean, it has something to do with age and maturity, doesn't it?

Bill Well, some people, even as children, have that understanding, and others never have it.

Pat How do you feel about the way men's and women's relationships are normally shown on TV?

Bill It's pretty hard for me to say much about that, because I find it hard to watch most of the stuff you see on TV. As I see it, the main problem is that women are only very rarely seen doing anything serious on TV, and I think that's really a reflection of the way women are regarded in society. I mean, if in society, in life, people feel that when something meaningful is being done, it's going to be a man doing it, we can hardly blame the TV if it reflects that attitude. It's up to us all to work on the attitude and change it.

Pat Actually you're making me think of those programmes where the women don't do much more than stand around smiling vacantly or pouring coffee or offering emotional support while the man does things.

Bill But worse than that in my opinion is news programmes where the women reporters get pushed into mainly domestic reporting while the men get to all the exciting 'meaningful' places. The fact is that the rules in society are set by men and I really think we're going to have to wait till substantial numbers of women achieve positions of power before there can be any radical change in the situation.

Pat But you do hear about more women in top management positions nowadays, don't you?

Bill I do think things are going in the right direction, yes, but of course it's going to take a long time before the woman's experience is given its full value by the men around her. Men are quite simply unaccustomed to trying to see things through a woman's eyes. There are a whole lot of things in life which . . . well, let me say, in my job in television I very often get scripts from women, and I see bits of the script, behaviour, experiences of life, which could only occur to a woman, and since TV is largely a man's world, it's often those bits that go out in the editing rooms because the men don't understand them . . .

Unit 9
Speeches

Activity 1

Well . . . I'm afraid, sorry to interrupt the party, but as I'm sure we're all aware . . . as I'm sure we're all aware, we're gathered here this afternoon for what is at the same time the happy and sad purpose of saying a sincere farewell to Beth Hopkins, who's leaving us for . . . higher things after twelve years' hard work in the country, I mean in this *company*. I hope that you all, and above all you Beth, will forgive me if I take this opportunity on this occasion of saying one or two words, or maybe a few hundred . . . about Beth's contribution to this company, because, she's the sort of quiet, unassuming worker whose contribution all too often goes unnoticed in the rush and stress of company life, and I feel it's only fair on an occasion like this, before I pass on the farewell gifts I've been asked to . . . pass to you from us all, Beth . . . if I draw attention to some of the things you've done, to show you that they *have* been noticed, and that you're leaving behind . . . much more than the memory of a thoroughly pleasant colleague, sorry . . .

When Beth arrived to take over this department, the relationship between management and staff was pretty bad . . . there was a very clear feeling of them-and-us, a separation . . . and very little staff participation in decision-making. It was also true that management then considered that Beth's job was to carry out their decisions, and that she should not do anything on her own initiative. And it is a measure of Beth's success in her job that she has, over the years, quietly shown, quietly persuaded management to listen to her, to the point where it would now be unthinkable for any management decision to be made concerning this department, in any way, without in-depth consultations with Beth, who could always be relied on to' know your general feelings about things. And at the same time . . . and at the same time as she was winning the respect and admiration of management, she's worked hard and diplomatically to bring . . . staff, yourselves into the decision-making process, to make your voice heard at management level, and the fact that she has succeeded in this is no mean feat. I'll give you just one example. In questions of design, it had always been company policy to buy in design ideas from outside experts, you know, specialists, but in the last few years, and almost entirely as a result of Beth's insistence . . . about it . . . that policy has been reversed and something like half the design ideas we have incorporated into our products in recent years have come from inside the company, many from you in this department. And as I say, that's just one example. I could give you many more . . .

In closing, too, I should just like to refer to a few of the things that Beth never let us know about herself, because they show what sort of a person she is when she's not here, when she was here, well, you know what I mean . . . Like her work for handicapped children in the area . . . she's an area organiser of the fund-raising campaigns . . . I found that out, by the way, when I heard her interviewed on the local radio one day . . . and the fact that she's an accomplished singer with the local Orpheus choir. Beth, you're full of surprises, and we shall miss you a lot . . . But we shouldn't be selfish, our loss is somebody else's gain, and I'm sure I'm speaking for all of us when I say we wish you all the very best in your new job and hope that this . . . small offering from us will bring back happy memories of your time with the company . . .

Activity 2

MP	. . . So let me make it quite clear . . . although the state of the rivers in this country has improved greatly during the last few years, while my party has been in power, and though we can now honestly say that more than 98% of our rivers are habitable for fish . . .
Heckler	Has anyone asked the fish?
MP	and habitable for other forms of wild life
Heckler	like MPs!
MP	I am afraid there are still two percent of our rivers that contain dangerous and of course illegal levels of contamination. My Ministry has taken severe measures to improve things, but in spite of these measures, and in spite of the very high fines imposed on those companies that break the law, there are still some people in this beautiful country of ours who would rather break the law and pay a fine than spend some money on cleaning up their factories. And I say to those selfish and irresponsible law-breakers that under my new law, which my party will make sure will be strictly and impartially enforced . . . under my new law, those law-breakers, whoever they are, whatever they manufacture, and however important the factory is in the community, they will have to clean up their factories or go to prison, whether they like it or not . . .

Unit 10
The Past

Activity 1

Part 1

Britain had food rationing from January 1940, beginning with bacon, ham, butter and meat. The butter ration was 100 grams (later 50 grams) a week; cheese varied from 20–25 grams; eggs one per fortnight if you were lucky (but expectant mothers and children under five got as many as three a week); two kinds of milk powder, skimmed and National Dried (full cream); tea, 50 grams a week, but more for old-age pensioners; sugar 350 grams, but more in the jam-making season. There was a 'points' system for canned foods (most of which came from America or the Dominions) cereals and condensed milk. Sweets (50 grams a week) came on personal points: there was a lot of propaganda about how bad they were for the teeth. From America, too, came spam (spiced ham) and dried eggs. From April 1942, there was a national loaf of bread. No onions. No bananas. No oranges except for children. Expectant mothers had green ration books ('Eat for one and a bit,' said the radio doctor in his homely way) and orange juice and vitamins A and D. They were not supposed to share their good fortune with the rest of the family, but . . . They were also allowed to jump the endless, day-long queues at food shops.

Part 2

If you were invited to dine or stay at anyone's house you took your rations with you in disgusting little sticky packages. Part of the social revolution of the war was that British housewives, servantless and sharpened by rationing, began to be really good cooks. This began modestly enough by following the government advice on making the best of too little food. The Ministry of Food was headed by an organisational genius, Fred Marquis, Baron Woolton. He gave friendly little morning radio talks on 'The Kitchen Front' and made housewives feel heroic. Propaganda characters appeared – Mr Carrot and Potato Pete. It was patriotic to eat more potatoes than bread because most wheat was imported. Carrots, people were told, helped you to see in the blackout, like Cats Eyes Cunningham, the RAF pilot who had shot down so many planes at night. Civilians did not yet know that Cats Eyes had radar to help him. Eat carrot flan. Make a cake out of flour, custard powder and dried egg. Liquid paraffin was available for medicinal purposes, but you could also use it as cooking fat. Learn about calories and proteins. Lord Woolton also invented, or at least gave his name to, Woolton Pie, which some people thought delicious and others thought dangerously stodgy; it was made of carrots, parsnips, turnips, potatoes, pastry and white sauce. Carrots were also the chief ingredient of wartime Christmas pudding.

Activity 2

In the 1960s talismans, charms, amulets and runic stones with wondrous powers abounded; a man would wear a copper bracelet to ward off rheumatism, for instance, and when he found that he did not contract rheumatism, took this as a triumphant vindication of the efficacy of the device. Another, no less insistent on his rationality, would fit a short length of steel chain to the back of his motor car; this dangled down and touched the ground as the car sped along, and was supposed to ward off car sickness, as the bracelet rheumatism. What such things had in common was a pseudo-scientific basis; this gave the believer a feeling of superiority over the heathen who, in his blindness, bows down to wood and stone, which, as everybody knows, are powerless to affect the lives of men, unlike copper bracelets and lengths of steel chain. It amounted to a search for certainty, for reassurance. All ages have searched for such things, but never had there been such an age as this for dismissing as false conclusions the certainties and reassurances found in previous times. Orthodox religion would not do; authority – political, moral, parental, pedagogical – would not do. What *would* do? The market-place resounded with rival claims; the interesting difference in the case of the 60s, as opposed to the market-place of earlier times, being that now it was the buyers, rather than the sellers, who were shouting the wares.

It happened in small things as well as large. A tiny clue was provided by the sudden rush, during the decade, to buy foods believed to be more wholesome, because more 'natural', than the buyers' customary fare. Far from being the province of a small and dedicated band, the shops selling natural foods, or 'health' foods, as they were called, began to be patronised by ever-growing numbers of people, and the numbers of the shops themselves began in consequence to multiply, eventually springing up in almost every neighbourhood, and even, in some cases, being run by the same proprietors as the chains of food-stores which had done so much to turn people away from the processed food they sold in the direction of the natural.

In the big things, of course, it happened even more. Much faith was placed in gurus of all kinds, though the turnover was rapid as the certainties they offered proved to be temporary, and the convictions they carried, brief. A Canadian professor, Marshall McLuhan, offered a new world-view, declaring in a succession of books that the printed word was finished. Enthusiastically taken up, on both sides of the Atlantic, by those whose business it was to spot new trends, and, when unable to spot any, to create them, McLuhan became a party game . . . Soon many were to be heard decrying linear thinking, speaking of tactile values, and dividing media into cool and hot. Beneath it all there could be clearly sensed the desire of the customers to be told that there was a clue to the world and that McLuhan had found it . . .

Unit 11
Leisure and education

Activity 1

. . . All right? Well, the basis of my . . . workshop today is a study I made some time ago of the leisure habits, of people's leisure habits, according to their age groups, sex, etcetera, and what I'd like to do in this preliminary session is give you the facts and figures, as it were, for one particular age-group and get you to jot down the figures and analyse them to see if you can explain . . . how people use their leisure time . . . see if you can explain the statistics, in other words.

Now the age group I'm going to take is the 20s to 30s, and I'm going to give you the figures for three categories, namely, married with no children, and married with children . . . and I'm going to kick off by talking about women. So just to recap, we're talking about women in the 20–30 age bracket, okay? And perhaps you can build up a table with those three categories, right? This'll be a bit dry, all figures, but once you've got them down I think you'll find the exercise quite amusing.

Now there are six things that tend to occupy women's time more, spare time I mean, after they're married. Not surprisingly, perhaps, TV is one of them. Single women average 10.7% of their leisure time on it, while for marrieds without children the figure grows to 14.2 and once the kids arrive it goes up to 19.8. Another fairly large rise comes in the category of crafts and hobbies, where the proportions rise from 11.6 for single women, to 18.6 after marriage and 20.7 with children. A slight rise now, in gardening: 0.3 – almost nothing – for the single girl, rising to 2.4 after marriage and 3.1 with children. Then excursions: 7% for single girls, rising to 8.4 after marriage and dropping back to 7.7 with children. A more substantial rise now, in what I call 'other activities', in which I included such things as further education, non-routine shopping, holidays and so on: 6.7 when you're single, 9.5 when you marry and 13.6 once the children arrive. Oh, am I going too fast? Sorry, sorry, I'll slow down a bit. Here's one you'll like, another rise, walking . . . yes, walking. 5.7 when you're single, down to 4.3 when you marry and up to 7.8 with children. I'll leave you to draw what conclusions you like from that one . . .

Now for the falls, okay? Active physical recreation, sport, etcetera, no less than 28% for single girls – that category includes dancing, swimming, horse-riding and skating, by the way – 28 for single girls, down to 15.4 after marriage and to 9.8 when the children come . . . And another big drop is in reading: 7.5 to 6.1 to 4.0. And in cinema- and theatre-going: 5.6 to 2.8 to 1.4 . . . And club activities: down too . . . the typical drama clubs, women's institutes, music societies, etcetera . . . down 5.3 to 3.2 to 1.8. Okay? A fairly insignificant drop now, in spectator sports, physical recreation as a spectator: 1.7, 1.7, then down to 1.0. Visits

to the pub, down a little too: 2.9 to 2.2 to 2.2. One final figure . . . are you still with me? . . . For social activities . . . 7% for single girls, an upsurge to 11.2% after marriage, then back down to 7% once the kids arrive . . . Right? Now I'll give you a bit of a breathing space before I go on to the men's figures, or perhaps I should say the figures for the men . . .

Activity 2

Right, well, now for the weaker sex . . . I think you'll find this quite revealing when you come to compare the two sets of figures. We're still with the same age-group, 20s to 30, sorry 20 to 30s, and now the men. Got that? Here we go. Now three areas tend to be fairly stable . . . Excursions, for example. They don't change at all: 8.7 in all three.

(**Female voice** Slackers . . .)

Spectator sports, from 2.4 down to 1.7, and then back up to 2.4 again. And the 'other activities' category: relatively stable, too, 11.8, down to 8.5, then back to 11.8 for a married man with children. Now for the big increases . . . TV . . . 10.3, 13.8, to 20.8 . . . Quite a rise in gardening, too: 1.3 to 3.4, then a rise to 6.2 . . . Crafts and hobbies have a slight rise, 4.2 to 5.6, and then stays the same. Sorry, am I going too fast again? . . . In the section I called 'maintenance', which includes jobs for the house and the car – that doesn't appear in the women's figures, that section – that rises, in fact, quite sharply, 3.9 to 10.9 and then drops back to, it drops back to 8.8. Now for one that might surprise you. Walking. Romeo, unmarried, 2%

(**Female voice** To the pub and back . . .)

Romeo, married with no children, 4.8. Romeo, with children, down to 4.1.

(**Female voice** Who takes the kids for a walk then?)
(**Male voice** And the dog?)

Then there's a slight rise in social activities: 2.7 to 4.1 and then a drop to 3.4. Okay? Are you still with me? Not far to go now.

Now for the falls. Well, as with the women, the reading goes down: 6.5 to 5.6 to 3.7. So does the cinema- and theatre-going: from 3.3 to 2.6 to 1.2. And so do club activities, initially: from 6.4 to 2.9 after marriage but rising again when the kids arrive to 4.3.

(**Female voice** Skiving off . . .)

Drop in active physical recreation, as well, though not so bad as for women: 24.2 to 22.1 to 15.1. And the biggest drop of all, can you imagine what that was?

(**Female voice** Compliments to the woman? . . .)

In fact, in visits to pubs and bars. Single men waste 12.3% of their leisure time in pubs, believe it or not, but I am happy to say that under our benign influence, we manage to reduce this waste of time and money to 5.3% in the first instance, and finally to 3.9 once they become mature and responsible . . .

Unit 12
Advertisements

Activity 1

Tricia   Hey, did you phone up about that flat?

Val   Phone? I've been to see the thing.

Tricia   No good?

Val   A real rip-off. £175 a month, for a start, and a greasy landlord. The shifty sort that make your flesh creep.

Tricia   Oh, charming.

Val   I think every single thing in the ad was fiction. I mean, well just look at the ad . . . yes, here. First floor, they say. It wasn't. It's an old terraced house, and they've done a conversion job, and they've got this flat in the cellar, right. and then for this flat, the one in the ad, you go up the front steps and in the front door and there you are, so it's the ground floor really. And it's not self-contained either, because the people in the real first floor flat, upstairs use the staircase . . . so you've got no privacy really. Prize location? Huh! Across the road from a disco, and next-door to a Chinese restaurant, in a one-way street with heavy traffic.

Tricia   Honestly! How dare they put all that stuff in the ad?

Val   At first I thought I'd got the wrong address.

Tricia   It was at least in Cadogan Walk, was it?

Val   Yes, that at least. Large reception room! If that was large I'm a battery hen. It was tiny! But tiny! Just about enough room for two people to sit down. And they said the colour TV was being repaired, but the only place you could have put it was hanging from the ceiling.

Tricia   Sounds like a flat for dwarfs.

Val   Yes, really. Two bedrooms? Well, there were two square boxes where you could probably put a bed, if you cut off the head and foot, but you wouldn't be able to have any furniture. And the slightly bigger one, the one they called a double, had the wall-paper peeling and rising damp . . . and the small one had a window that didn't open.

Tricia   Incredible.

Val   Then what? Diner? Didn't see it. Newly-fitted kitchen? Well, there was a kitchen but . . .

Tricia   Newly-fitted with Victorian-style fittings?

Val   Yes. Rusty taps and a table with a piece missing.

Tricia   And the garden?

Val   A bit of grass, a bit of mud, an old bicycle and some dead pot plants. You could hardly see it.

Tricia   No garage either I suppose.

Val   Oh, yes . . . but £40 a month extra.

Tricia   Gas central heating?

Val   I wouldn't dare light a match in that building, let alone trust gas.

Tricia   Sunny?

Val   Five minutes a day, if you're lucky. The house next door has got three floors and it's a narrow street with trees.

Tricia   And close to tubes, buses and shops . . .?

Val   So close it's like having them in your front room.

Tricia   Well, I take it we're not going to live there then?

Val   What do you think?

Activity 2

Mark   Hello, Weybridge 4153.

Peter   Oh hello. I was just calling about . . . about that 2001 car you were advertising in today's paper. Could you explain a bit about what it's actually got . . . what all the stuff on the ad means . . .

Mark   Yes, sure. It's my invention, you see. I based it on a drawing I saw in the *Sunday Times* a couple of years ago, and I've incorporated all the new technology into one car, which, incidentally, is why it's . . . rather expensive.

Peter   Yes, it's not exactly what one would pay for a Mini, is it? . . . For example, what are . . . 'corn. lamps'?

Mark   Ah, yes. Cornering lamps. They are headlamps that swivel round, turn round according to the degree of turn on the steering wheel . . . adapting to the bends so you're never left blind.

Peter   And I take it that 'rains sens. wipers' means rain-sensitive wind-screen wipers, does it?

Mark   That is the full name, indeed. Those are wipers that are sensitive to moisture. So as soon as they feel moisture they come on automatically.

Peter   Ingenious. And why the choice of 2 or 4 cylinders?

Mark   Fuel economy. That is, if for any reason you don't want the full power of the engine, of the 4 cylinders, then you can switch off two of them and the car's perfectly happy.

Peter   And this 'remote-control door-locking system'?

Mark   That's a bit of a gimmick, actually. It uses an infra-red ray, like the remote control on your TV set. Press a button at a distance and your door locks.

Peter   I suppose the plastic panels are for lightness, are they?

Mark   Yes, yes. They cost me the earth to get hold of, too. They're used in building aircraft. Incredibly light, hardly feel the weight.

Peter   And what about this thing of 'twin tyres'?

Mark   Yes, that's a safety idea really. If you get a puncture in one you can drive on quite safely on the other. Nylon-steel radials.

Peter   What?

Mark   Nice little jobs. Last ages.

Peter   Oh. And the 4-wheel steering? Is that like on a jeep or a Land-Rover?

Mark	Oh bless you no. That's what it says. You can steer the rear wheels as well. That's really for parking in confined spaces.
Peter	But doesn't that make the car rather unstable?
Mark	No . . . it combines the two essential virtues of complete stability at high speeds with low-speed manoeuvrability.
Peter	Then I see it has optional settings for the power-assisted steering.
Mark	Indeed it has.
Peter	If it's not a rude question, what's the use of that?
Mark	Simple, really. Some drivers don't like too much power-assistance, so what I've done is make it optional . . . you fix the amount of power assistance you want.
Peter	Oh . . . What about the navigation system?
Mark	Well, there's a computer on board. You program your route into the computer, and the computer reminds you which turnings to take and when.
Peter	It speaks, does it?
Mark	With an impeccable BBC accent.
Peter	What will they think of next?
Mark	Sorry?
Peter	This . . . this 'drowsiness monitor' . . .?
Mark	Same computer. You record a program with your normal driving patterns, and the computer reminds you when you deviate from those patterns.
Peter	I can understand the anti-lock brakes – that's self-explanatory – but this 'automatic suspension adjustment' . . . I thought all cars had that.
Mark	Oh goodness no. This system – it's really my masterpiece – it's a system, the first in the world that adapts automatically to the condition of the road surface you happen to be on. It even works on rough mountain tracks.
Peter	Only trouble with this car is it's so expensive.
Mark	Yes, but you see it's been lovingly assembled with my own fair hands, it's a fantastically advanced machine . . . only three of them built so far, so you won't see your neighbour with one, at least, not unless you . . .
Peter	Yes, well, thank you very much. You've been most helpful. Bye.
Mark	Genius is never appreciated.

Unit 13
Behind superstitions

Activity 1

Now there is one quite extraordinary piece of evidence which suggests that shape could be important in receiving even cosmic stimuli. And that is the Pyramids of Egypt. The pyramids on the west bank of the Nile were built by the pharaohs as royal tombs and date from about 3000 BC. The most celebrated are those at Giza, built during the Fourth Dynasty, of which the largest is the one that housed the pharaoh Khufu, better known as Cheops – which is now called the Great Pyramid.

Now, some years ago it was visited by a Frenchman named Bovis who took refuge from the midday sun in the pharaoh's chamber which is situated in the centre of the pyramid exactly one third up from the base. He found it unusually humid there, but what really surprised him were the garbage cans that contained, among the usual tourist litter, the bodies of a cat and some small desert animals that had wandered into the pyramid and died there. Despite the humidity none of them had decayed, but just dried out like mummies. He began to wonder whether the pharaohs had really been so carefully embalmed by their subjects after all, or whether there was something about the pyramids themselves that preserved bodies in a mummified condition. Bovis made an accurate scale model of the Cheops pyramid, and placed it like the original with the base lines facing precisely north–south and east–west. Inside the model, one third of the way up, he put a dead cat. It became mummified, and he concluded that the pyramid promoted rapid dehydration.

Reports of this discovery attracted the attention of Karel Drbal, a radio engineer in Prague, who repeated the experiment with several dead animals and concluded, 'There is a relation between the shape of the space inside the pyramid and the physical, chemical and biological processes going on inside that space. By using suitable forms and shapes, we should be able to make processes occur faster or delay them.' Drbal remembered an old superstition which claimed that a razor left in the light of the moon became blunted. He tried putting one under his model pyramid, but nothing happened, so he went on shaving with it until it was blunt, and then put it back in the pyramid. It became sharp again.

Getting a good razor-blade is still difficult in many Eastern European countries, so Drbal tried to patent and market his discovery. The patent office in Prague refused to consider it until their chief scientist had tried building a model himself and found that it worked. So the Cheops Pyramid Razor-blade Sharpener was registered in 1959 under the Czechoslovakian Republic Patent No. 91304, and a factory soon began to turn out miniature cardboard pyramids.

Today they make them in styrofoam.

The edge of a razor-blade has a crystal structure. Crystals are almost alive, in that they grow by reproducing themselves. When a blade becomes blunted, some of the crystals on the edge, where they are only one layer thick, are rubbed off. Theoretically, there is no reason why they should not replace themselves in time. We know that sunlight has a field that points in all directions, but sunlight reflected from an object such as the moon is partly polarised, vibrating mostly in one direction. This could conceivably destroy the edge of a blade left under the moon, but it does not explain the reverse action of the pyramid. We can only guess that the Great Pyramid and its little imitations act as lenses that focus energy, or as resonators that collect energy which encourages crystal growth. The pyramid shape itself is very much like that of a crystal of magnetite, so perhaps it builds up a magnetic field. I do not know the answer, but I do know that it works. My record so far with Wilkinson Sword blades is four months of continuous daily use. I have a feeling that the manufacturers are not going to like the idea very much . . .

Activity 2

Dogs, it seems are the best UFO detectors, and dislike them intensely. Some of them bark, some howl, and some froth in terror when an object is about. And all these reactions are elicited before humans are aware of anything unusual. It may be a high-pitched sound which alerts them, or it may be microwave transmissions, but the chances are that the phenomenon is as variable for them as it is for us. At the time Jung wrote his paper, in 1958, he did not have access to the wealth of quantitative material. He concluded nevertheless that 'we are dealing with an ostensibly physical phenomenon, distinguished on the one hand by its strange, unknown, and indeed contradictory nature'. And he decided that the evidence could support one of two hypotheses, 'In the first case, an objectively real, physical process forms the basis for an accompanying myth; in the second a psychological archetype creates the corresponding vision'. Nobody will be surprised to learn that he came down in favour of the latter.

Jung called the UFO reports 'variations on a visionary rumour', and likened them to the collective visions experienced by crusaders during the siege of Jerusalem, by troops at Mons in the First World War, and by the faithful gathered to see the Virgin at Fatima in Portugal. And he reasoned, 'If it is a case of psychological projection, there must be a psychic cause for it. One can hardly suppose that anything of such world-wide incidence as the UFO legend is purely fortuitous and of no importance whatsoever.' He was particularly impressed by the fact that so many witnesses were not expecting to see anything, had no previous belief in UFOs, and were in general characters renowned for their cool judgement and critical reason. 'In just these cases,' he observed triumphantly, 'the unconscious mind has to resort to particularly drastic measures in order to make its contents perceived. It does this most vividly by projection, by extrapolating its contents into an object, which then reflects back what had previously lain hidden in the unconscious.' He went on to suggest that such individuals were involved in a collective experience because a political, social, philosophical and religious conflict of unprecedented proportion has split the consciousness of our age. Jung believed that tension of this kind created a 'potential' which often expressed itself in a manifestation of energy. He had sound personal reasons for holding such a belief because in 1909 in an altercation with Freud a loud detonation had occurred in a bookcase at their side; closely followed, when Jung, who felt a great inner certainty about it, said 'I now predict that in a moment there will be another loud report' . . . by a second similar explosion. And because most of the UFOs known to him were saucers, discs, cylinders or spheres, Jung interpreted them as symbols of unity and wholeness, rising spontaneously out of the unconscious to provide a focus for healing . . .

Unit 14
The language of argument

Activity 1

Simon Well, Professor, the obligatory question to begin with really is that here we are in the year 1985, 1984 has come and gone, and, well, George Orwell's prophecy has not come true, has it?

Professor Oh, I think one has to be a bit careful before one makes statements like that, you know. I think that if we take the fictional year of 1984 *literally*, we would in fact be guilty of a fallacy.

Simon What sort of fallacy?

Professor Well, it's rather like that first cosmonaut . . . wasn't it Gagarin . . . the one in the first Sputnik in 1957, who said, when he was out there in space, that he couldn't see God . . .

Simon He couldn't see God out there in space?

Professor Yes, and therefore, he said, therefore God didn't exist.

Simon Which is the fallacy of . . .?

Professor Well, the fallacy there, of course, is that he was presupposing that the God religious people believe in was some sort of *visible* human-like being flying around out there in space . . .

Simon . . . which is of course a distortion, a fallacy . . .

Professor Yes, because I don't think you'd find many believers who would have that idea of God. But you see, for him, for Gagarin, coming from a state with a materialist ideology, it was a way of . . . *reducing* the idea of religion to an absurdity, mocking it, to follow the line of the prevailing ideology in his country.

Simon Reducing it to an absurdity to discredit it.

Professor Yes indeed.

Simon He made a bit of a fool of himself, didn't he then, Gagarin?

Professor Ah, but hang on a minute. There you are reducing Gagarin to an absurdity to discredit him. But fallacies like that make fools of us all – we're all prone to make them.

Simon And if we say Orwell was wrong about the date, what fallacy is that?

Professor Well, I think we are guilty of distorting Orwell's *intention* with his title *Nineteen Eighty-Four*. I'm sure he never meant the year *literally*. We have to remember that he was writing in the post-war 1940s, and what he meant by choosing 1984, was a year in the not-too-distant future in which, if the political trends he saw in the post-war years continued, his prophecies would come true.

Simon So he chose 1984 to give the prophecy a sense of urgency, sort of like saying, 'this is going to happen very soon if you're not careful'.

Professor That's it. And the other fallacy that comes when you try to discredit it by taking the title too literally is that you forget that any profound work of literature requires constant re-interpretation. I mean by that that the way we interpret *Nineteen Eighty-Four* today is not the same as we would have done in 1964 or 1954. There is no definitive interpretation of any real work of art because times change, and with them our ways of thinking and seeing.

Simon But *Nineteen Eighty-Four* does have its faults, doesn't it?

Professor Yes, of course, but there, if I may say so, you are guilty of another fallacy. I'm not suggesting that *Nineteen Eighty-Four* is a perfect work of art. I'm simply saying that *any* work of art should be taken on its own terms, and that means we have to make a very serious attempt to read *between* as well as on the lines . . . to try to understand the author's full meaning . . .

Activity 2

Section 1

Clare I wonder what the result of the election will be.

Brian Well, I hope the country will have the common sense to vote for a sound and sensible business government, I must say. What this country needs is a period of peace and quiet, so that it can get back on the road to prosperity. Oh, another cup of coffee, Clare? Clare, you know, Philip, calls herself a Socialist, but this time I trust you'll vote Conservative, Clare.

Clare As a matter of fact, as a scientist I find myself in disagreement with all political parties. They all seem to me to be equally unscientific. The vital problems of finding outlets for our expanding population, and of sorting out the unfit can only be solved by the application of the scientific method to political problems. At present, I see no signs of any of the political parties realising this, so this time I've taken the decision that I'm not going to vote.

Section 2

Philip Well, as a clergyman, a minister of the Gospel, it seems to me that the great problem before us is the lifting-up of the labouring masses . . .

Brian The working classes, you mean?

Philip Yes . . . Now I put my trust in an enlightened and Christianised Socialism. I realise very well that our Labour Party is not ideal, but, purified from its materialism . . .

Brian But what you don't realise, my dear chap, is that the

Labour Party's aims are materialist through and through. Fill the worker's stomach, make him comfortable, and forget his soul. You can't call that Christianity. There wouldn't be any room for clergymen in the Socialist State!

Clare I've got no objection to filling people's stomachs. I mean, we've eaten well tonight, and we're the better for it. I should fill every worker's stomach, but stop this business of robbing the people who work hard to support the idle and inefficient. Well, that's unbiological.

Section 3

Brian And the workers themselves will be the first to suffer when the country is ruined . . . look at the level of income tax now. It was private enterprise that built up the industrial system that gave us our prospertiy. That's what we must get back to if we want the country to prosper again.

Philip No person should be content with our industrialism while one child living under that system is short of food.

Brian Philip, my dear chap, no one wants children to starve. Industrialism does more towards feeding children than all the socialist theories in the world. How many children does the Labour Party feed?

Philip I've not got much respect for any particular political party, but I expect the Labour Party does as much or as little in direct relief of poverty as any other political party.

Section 4

Clare Let's go back to a point in the argument which interests me more than the merits or demerits of the Labour Party. You both seem to agree that children should not be starving, but as a scientist I can't agree with you there.

Philip My goodness . . . I'd have thought we'd agree on that at least . . .

Clare You'll see what I mean in a minute. You see, Nature effects all improvements in the human race by a process of elimination of the unfit, by natural selection. By natural selection, the horse has become strong and the greyhound fast. You see, scientifically speaking, starvation is one of Nature's weapons for eliminating the unfit. The sight of her methods may offend our humaner feelings, but the attempt of sentimental philanthropy to interfere with them can only lead to degeneration of the human race. A State-subsidised national health service which keeps alive the children of the unfit is a biological crime.

Unit 15
Points of view

Activity 1

Stella Hello . . . hello . . . next caller please . . . are you there?

Mr Clarke Oh yes . . .

Stella Who's that speaking please?

Mr Clarke This is Cuthbert Clarke here, from Magnolia Road, Pyecraft.

Stella Yes, Mr Clarke, and what's your protest about, actually?

Mr Clarke About . . . abuses in health food stores, you see . . .

Stella Abuses in health foods stores, Mr Clarke? What sort of abuses?

Mr Clarke Well, my main complaint, and I know I'm not alone in feeling this . . . there are certain chains of health foods shops where they guarantee that the foods they sell have been . . . organically grown and don't contain any . . . additives at all.

Stella I thought all health food stores guaranteed that. No additives I mean.

Mr Clarke Well, they do up to a point, but there is a difference you see between health food that is industrially produced and that which is produced in relatively small quantities by biologically sound processes. Now, in the latter type of products, there is some justification for prices being higher, but in my opinion, the prices of these products . . .

Stella That is, the prices of the foods produced by biologically sound processes?

Mr Clarke That's it, yes, . . . the prices of those products, in my opinion, in the 'Rising Sun' chain of healthfood stores, are outrageous.

Stella Can you give us some examples please, Mr Clarke?

Mr Clarke Of course, I have a list here. For instance, a 1 lb jar of honey. Now, you can buy guaranteed unadulterated honey in a supermarket for about £1 a jar . . . but in the 'Rising Sun' shops, a honey that tastes and looks exactly the same except for the labels and guarantee would cost you double. The same happens with jams, rice, shampoos, a lot of things. I'm not at all doubting the quality of the 'Rising Sun' products, mind. Only the price mark-up. I think 100% is ridiculous.

Stella But the customer does have a choice, Mr Clarke. Surely, if people are prepared to pay those prices in the 'Rising Sun' shops it's because they want to, because they recognise quality when they see it.

Mr Clarke Yes, up to a point, but there's a principle involved, you see. The majority of people who buy their food in healthfood stores do so because they're ill or on a special diet, or both, and this makes them vulnerable, because it makes them prepared to pay any price – you know, because of the feeling that it's silly to count the cost when you're ill . . .

Activity 2

Anne Well, another lunchtime demonstration in the city centre outside city hall . . . a lot of traffic disruption, but no trouble, arrests, or untoward incidents. And with us in the studio we've got one of the organisers of the demo . . .

Matt I'd prefer to be introduced as 'one of the organising *committee*' if you don't mind. Less personal, if you see what I mean.

Anne Sorry . . . one of the organising committee, then . . . Mr Matt Sutcliffe.

Matt I requested that change because we are not a few agitators and troublemakers who decided to organise a demonstration, which is what some of the media would like the general public to believe, but an organising committee representing a very widespread movement of protest . . . the demand for a demo came as a result of democratic processes.

Anne Could you explain briefly what the demonstration was for?

Matt Basically we are concerned about the closure of the Tellmark factory, which is going to throw 300 people out of work, in a city where the unemployment rate is already in advance of 14%, which is way above the national average. But what we are also aiming at is what lies behind this closure, namely the Government's so-called 'Industrial Reorganisation Programme', which seems to us, to us in the protest movement, to be sacrificing human beings at the altar of economic expediency.

Anne You think there was no real need for the factory to be closed?

Matt If one thinks of the factory solely in terms of balance sheets, of profits and losses, there are of course convincing reasons for closing it, but our argument is that a responsible government ought to have the intelligence, the moral sense, and the political insight and foresight to look beyond the short term, beyond the financial gains and losses, and see that if 300 jobs are to be cut, there should be some workable alternative available . . . particulary in a small industrial city like this.

Anne And what alternatives would you suggest?

Matt If there has to be reorganisation – and we do accept there has to be – there should in the first place be better provision of loans so that factories in difficulties can at least have a chance to get over a bad patch. Secondly, we believe that in areas where a lot of reorganisation is taking place, the Government should promote investment possibilities, so that new industries can get established and replace the failing ones. And thirdly, at the same time as these new industries are promoted, the Government should organise retraining schemes to help workers in failing industries to retrain for posts in new ones . . .

Unit 16
A roof over your head

Activity 1

I remember the most asymmetrical flat I ever saw, flat lay-out I mean . . . well, the structure too, because it was the walls that were funny, really . . . was in the African town where I was working . . . and the thing was . . . thanks . . . the thing was, it was a building that somehow . . . it was built on a smallish ledge of rock just below the old Turkish walls of the town, and it had to be asymmetrical because, well, rocks are asymmetrical, so, so none of the walls were in a straight line, know what I mean? So, I mean you entered up some little steps from the street and you found yourself in a patio . . . I mean there was a double gate and the patio was walled so you felt really private . . . shut in . . . and . . . the only rooms opening directly onto the patio were the kitchen and the WC, which were pretty tiny, too, actually, and both about the same size. And then there was the water tap over by the kitchen . . . that was the only water, by the way, so the guys who lived there had fitted a hose and nozzle to it to make it into a shower. Anyway, anyway . . . about five steps away, and you'd find yourself in what was called the sitting room, which could hold about four people comfortably . . . Now the funny thing was, and I didn't realise it till Dave, one of the guys who lived there, pointed it out to me, the funny thing was that the two walls, the wall on the side where all the windows and doors were, and the wall opposite . . . I mean I suppose you'd expect them to be straight, wouldn't you, or if not straight at least parallel, but they weren't you see, they both sloped, quite gently, almost imperceptibly, in different directions, the left-hand, window side, outwards, and the other side sloped the other way, so in fact the rooms got steadily wider as you went along . . .

Activity 2

Jane	Hello, Villa Service Holidays. Can I help you?
Mrs Wilson	Oh yes, yes, I was just calling about your ad here in the paper . . . about the holiday houses in France. This one about the chateau on the Loire . . . is that just a publicity gimmick or something?
Jane	Oh no, madam, it's true. We've got three chateaux on the list actually, and they're each divided into three self-contained houses.
Mrs Wilson	Jolly original, I must say.
Jane	And they really are beautifully furnished and equipped.
Mrs Wilson	Could you give me a few details, then, please?
Jane	I could send you a free brochure, madam, if you like . . .
Mrs Wilson	Oh yes, that too please, or no, no, no, no . . .

	I'll drop into your office and pick one up so don't bother . . . it's just to know, you know, more or less the costs and how many rooms and so forth.
Jane	Well, the most attractive of all really is the Chateau Lafitte . . . that's one with two towers actually and a central bit, so in fact the three houses are the two towers and the bit in the middle, all self-contained.
Mrs Wilson	We'll need a fair number of bedrooms because we'll have friends coming in you see. Quite a mob of us.
Jane	Well, just to give you an idea . . . each tower has three double bedrooms and two singles – one single's quite small in fact, but the other could be converted to sleep two comfortably, because it's got a camp bed . . .
Mrs Wilson	Hmmm, yes. So the whole house could at most sleep how many?
Jane	Eight or possibly nine.
Mrs Wilson	How about the other rooms?
Jane	There's a fully-equipped kitchen which can be used as a breakfast room, two bathrooms, and a full dining-sitting-room.
Mrs Wilson	And how much does one have to pay for all this?
Jane	What time would you want to be there, madam?
Mrs Wilson	Not absolutely sure actually . . . End of August, last fortnight, probably.
Jane	Then what would be £652 a week.
Mrs Wilson	6–52. Yes. Well, that's not outrageous. That's about £1300 for two weeks, isn't it. How does that compare with the house on the Cote d'Azur that you're advertising?
Jane	There's not a great deal of difference in the rental, madam.
Mrs Wilson	Have you got anything down there roughly the same size?
Jane	There's a lovely house in Sainte Maxime, madam. Sleeps eight.
Mrs Wilson	Sainte Maxime. I suppose one ought to know where that is, I'm afraid I don't.
Jane	It's a sort of satellite town near St Tropez, madam . . . Very pleasant . . . it has its own
	character, and it's not at all spoilt yet.
Mrs Wilson	Sounds all right. How about the house?
Jane	It's four kilometres from Sainte Maxime, with really lovely sea views, a big garden and a swimming-pool.
Mrs Wilson	Which the chateau didn't have, of course.
Jane	No, but at the chateau you could have horse-riding included in the price.
Mrs Wilson	Horses? Hmmm, that would be very nice for the girls. Well, go on.
Jane	The house sleeps eight comfortably. Three large twin bedrooms, one with a self-contained bathroom and the other two share one. Then there's a twin bedroom with bunk beds with its own shower-room and WC.
Mrs Wilson	Uhuh.
Jane	All the bedrooms have french doors to the large upstairs terrace.
Mrs Wilson	Mm.
Jane	And then on the ground floor there's a beautifully-equipped kitchen, and a very spacious lounge-dining-room with an open fireplace and exposed beams, beautifully furnished.
Mrs Wilson	It sounds as though you've been there and liked it!
Jane	Actually I was there last winter on an inspection tour . . . It's a dream house, really. And only about ten minutes' walk down to the beach.
Mrs Wilson	And it's about the same price as the chateau, is it?
Jane	It's a wee bit more costly, madam . . . £712 a week.
Mrs Wilson	I see. Well, well look . . . I'll have to talk this over with my family and our friends.
Jane	Of course, madam. But wouldn't you like a full catalogue? . . . We've got lots of really beautiful houses on offer.
Mrs Wilson	Oh yes, that'd be super, yes. It'd save me coming in.
Jane	Could I have your name please?
Mrs Wilson	Yes. Melissa Wilson.
Jane	Uhuh. And the address?
Mrs Wilson	Wentworth Manor, West Drabble . . .

Unit 17
Inferences

Activity I

Section 1

Judy   Hello . . .

Mum   Hello, hello Judy . . .

Judy   Hello Mum! How nice to hear your voice!

Mum   Hmmm. It would be nice to hear yours a bit more often, I must say, just to show you remember you've got parents.

Judy   Well, I've been terribly busy recently, what with the exams and so on . . .

Mum   Too busy to pick up a phone and phone home? For all you care we could have had an accident.

Judy   I do care, of course Mum, it's just that I've been working very hard, really.

Mum   I don't think it takes much trouble or time to pick up a phone.

Judy   Well, for that matter, Mum, why didn't you phone me? I told you last time I was going to be doing exams, but nobody's called me to ask how they've been going.

Mum   You didn't tell me anything about any exams.

Section 2

Judy   Well, I told Dad, I distinctly remember. Didn't he tell you?

Mum   Not a word. Well, how did the exams go then?

Judy   A bit late now, isn't it? I don't think you care one way or the other.

Mum   You know what your father's like. He's hopeless about telling me things.

Judy   Anyway, Mum, have you called me up to wish me luck or give me a telling-off?

Mum   Really, Judy, you do sound nervy. That's stress, that is. Have you been getting enough sleep lately? Do you eat properly there? I can just picture you all there in that flat, living on coffee and cigarettes. I get very worried about your health, you know.

Judy   We're living quite sensibly and comfortably, thanks, Mum, and in fact none of us smoke.

Section 3

Mum   I suppose your old family house isn't good enough any more.

Judy   Oh, don't start that again, Mum. We're fine here, really.

Mum   We've redecorated your room, you know, ready for the summer.

Judy   Actually, I wanted . . . I wanted to talk to you about the summer.

Mum   You're not going to tell us now that you've made other plans, like last summer?

Judy   Well, for part of the time I'll be going to Greece with some friends.

Mum   There we go again! Your father will be disappointed.

Judy   But you won't, I suppose.

Mum   Of course I will, my dear, that goes without saying. Anyway, I suppose your old Dad and I should start getting used to the idea that . . . that you only come to us when you want something, or when all else fails . . .

Section 4

Judy   Honestly, Mum, this conversation is really getting nowhere. I'm sorry, and I've got an exam to prepare for this afternoon.

Mum   Oh, I'm sorry to have disturbed you. Next time I'll book an appointment with your secretary . . . Well, good luck with your . . . exams.

Judy   Thanks, Mum. Look, I'll give you a call this evening when it's over, okay?

Mum   All right dear . . . if you have a moment. We'll be in. Bye.

Judy   Bye Mum. Oh . . .

Activity 2

. . . The most striking single statement in this year's issue of *Social Trends*, the Government's annual fact-pack on the state of Britain, occurs on page 188. It records, without comment, that as the economy slid deeper into redundancy and recession, only 42% of households with an unemployed head had a car available for private motoring. In a volume that variously records elsewhere that three million people in the country are currently without work, that a clear majority of old-age pensioners, though tending to give up their pets, are now enjoying the benefits of central heating, and that sub-aqua diving is the fastest-growing outdoor leisure activity, that probably hits just about the right balance between complacent cheerfulness and apolcalyptic gloom.

In 1959, after all, just a quarter of a century ago, only 16% of families in the UK enjoyed access to personal motor transport of any kind. And that was when politicians like George Brown were agonising over 'the job gap' – the prospects that there would never be enough hands available for the tasks crying out to be done. There is little argument – and plenty of evidence in this survey – that many British citizens are going through a pretty bad time. Nearly 1.2 million breadwinners have not collected a proper pay-packet for over a year. Three million houses out of a total stock of 18 million are either totally unfit for habitation, lack basic amenities, or need repairs costing more than £7,000. Almost half the 1.9 million women who have passed their 65th birthday are now condemned to live alone – though only 20% of men, who tend on average to marry younger, longer-living wives, and are considerably better-placed for retirement companionship. And crime of all kinds is on the rise, more disruptive, and increasingly likely to go undetected (indeed even unrecorded). But all these things have to be kept in perspective. It is perfectly proper to deplore the fact that households hit by unemployment can typically spend only £109 a week, whereas those with members still in jobs have £160 to play with. It is equally reasonable though to remark that, allowing for inflation which has cut the value of the £ to 25p over the past decade, the equivalent of £109 in 1971 was rather more than the average income then being earned by people in full-time work. Certainly, there is data to support the 'two-nations' argument, postulating a Britain increasingly divided between the haves and have-nots. Few of those drawing supplementary benefit or family income supplement or on the dole would be in the two-or-more-cars category – unlike 41% of those in the professional and managerial groups – or among those who spend £500 a year or more on their holidays – which is the average for those earning more than £240 a week. But in other areas there is a surprising degree of egalitarianism. Few in any economic or social category can be excluded when 95% of households have a vacuum cleaner, 93% have a refrigerator, 79% a washing-machine, 97% a TV and four people out of five do their own decorating. One particularly encouraging statistic is that 68% of all elderly people now have access to a telephone – almost double the number of nine years ago. That probably helps to explain a sharp drop – more than a third – in the number of fatal accidents in the home . . .

Unit 18
Complaints

Activity 1

Section 1

Tina Oh, hello. It's you.

....

Tina Yes, I did. What on earth happened to you?

....

Tina Well, yes. I was there expecting you. I wondered what had happened.

....

Tina No, he wasn't there. He said he felt I knew far more about it than he did, and that we'd get more work done if he wasn't there. Oh, hang on a minute . . . (*turns off the radio*) Ah, that's better.

....

Tina Well, I must say it was rather, because, you know, I chose a table with a good view of the door, so I could be sure of seeing you come in, and I told the waiter I was expecting you . . . The thing is they know Alan and me well in that place, very well, and . . .

Section 2

....

Tina I did remind you yesterday, you know. And you wrote it down in your diary, in front of me last Friday.

....

Tina Diary or not, Ray, you wrote it down.

....

Tina Well, if there is another time I think we'd better fix it in some place outside, like, you know, some place in the centre of town . . . because . . . you see, you know how things are, a young woman sitting by herself in a restaurant gets strange looks, especially when the people around you know you're expecting a male companion who hasn't turned up. I don't like it, but that's the way the world is, still.

....

Tina Yes, I'm sure you would have enjoyed it. They've got a good range on the menu . . . and we could have had a good look at the project without any hurry. . . .Oh, anyway . . .

Section 3

....

Tina Well, these things happen, I suppose.

....

Tina Yes, well, maybe we can fix another time for next week, if you're free, at midday some day. Trouble is I was wanting to finalise things so I could present the completed thing on Monday morning, so you see it

was important to clear things with you now, but I see I'll have to go on with things without you.

....

Tina Yes, well, don't let's keep on about it. These things happen.

....

Tina Bye.

Activity 2

Section 1

Jim Hello, hello . . . that you Brian?

....

Jim No, from Milan.

....

Jim You know as well as I do why I'm here. About selling that video training series to that TV station here.

....

Jim Precisely. That one. To cut a very long story short, they don't want it.

....

Jim I know you thought they did, but who did you talk to in the station?

....

Jim Don't you think it might have been a good idea to talk to the people who actually buy the programmes? I mean, if somebody had taken the trouble to talk to them I could have been saved the journey.

....

Jim He says you were the one who started the ball rolling, you who fixed up my visit . . .

....

Jim He may be on the spot, but he says the business was organised above his head, by you.

Section 2

....

Jim Basically because they're not prepared to spend any money to adapt it to their needs, apart from dubbing it in Italian, or subtitling it. What they want is a few video masters of programmes that they can buy and broadcast with no complications. Apparently that's the way they do business. They buy their programmes from outside, even the news.

....

Jim Well, that's what you think. They say it's a regional station with a coverage of about seven million people, so they're not used to dealing with high figures. And they get an episode of stuff like *Dallas* for $50 a minute, so our price sounded ridiculous.

....

Jim All right, about $56 a minute, but then they'd have to spend another $50 a minute on adapting it properly.

Section 3

. . . .

Jim   Not without making nonsense of the whole idea behind the series. It's got to have a front-person, a lecturer. You can't just show the cassettes without explanation, as if it were something like *Dallas*. It's quite simply the wrong kind of material for what they need . . . and what I feel very strongly is that someone should have taken the trouble to find that out before I was dragged out from London.

. . . .

Jim   No, the only production facility they offered was to have a front-person give a short intro in Italian before the film, and a few short comments afterwards. That would have raised the costs for them by $10 a minute.

. . . .

Jim   Who did you speak to?

. . . .

Jim   Look, Brian, they're all very nice . . . there are probably 900 nice Italians working for the company, in fact all the people I've met in Milan have been very nice so far. It's just that nobody wants to buy the product.

. . . .

Jim   Yes, but was he or she a manager or a receptionist or a liftboy or a waitress in the canteen?

. . . .

Section 4

Jim   Anyway, now I'm here I'm going to make a full report because there seem to be two possibilities.

. . . .

Jim   First, if we want to make something local for Milan, we could try to get some financial backing here in Milan, pay for the adaptation to be done here, and then go back to the TV station to try and sell it. But that could only be sold here in Italy.

. . . .

Jim   Yes, and the other possibility would be to work on the adaptation in London and produce something we could sell in other countries. Get a front-person to do an intro and comment on it, and then stick in some good graphic sequences with questions.

. . . .

Jim   As a matter of fact, Brian, it's pouring with rain and I don't see the point of staying here any longer anyway . . .

Test I

First part

South African-born athlete Zola Budd makes her first track appearance in this country this afternoon when she runs in an invitation 3,000 metres race in Dartford, Kent. And American Mark Bly has a 3-stroke lead going into the third round of the Masters' Golf Tournament in Augusta, Georgia. Bly shot a second-round 66 for a 9-under-par total of 135. Tom Kite lies in second place on 138, with Britain's Nick Faldo tying in third position with Australian David Graham and American Ben Cranshaw . . . Tony Doyle is still the overall leader in the Raleigh International Cycle Race, now entering its final day, but Doyle has just three seconds to spare over Ireland's Martin Early. Early was second behind Denmark's Kim Ericson in yesterday's fifth stage from Doncaster to Alton Towers. The race ends in Sheffield this afternoon . . . From cycles to horses and we have 6 race meetings taking place today, on the flat at Newbury and Thirsk, while there's National Hunt racing over the sticks at Ayr, Huntingdon, Stratford and Bangor-on-Dee. Colin Turner's selections are at Newbury in the 2.30, number 2, Creggan Score, which is also the favourite, and in the 3.30, still in Newbury, number 9 Dazari . . . at Thirsk in the 3.15, number 5, Kraken Wake . . . at Stratford in the 3.00, number 8, Tamanrasset, and at Bangor-on-Dee, in the 2.30, number 5, Pearl. . . .A cricket flash now, latest score in the West Indian touring side's first game of the season, at Worcester. Worcestershire put in to bat after losing the toss, and staggering a bit in face of the West Indian pace attack . . . latest score we have is Worcestershire 73 for 4 . . . Flash for showjumping fans now, from the European championships in Amsterdam, Holland, where British champion Sandra Mapleson came back after yesterday's reverses and jumped faultlessly and fast to put herself back in the running for a medal. Not such good news for Britain's Derek Tyler, however. His horse Bleak House went lame after the first round and couldn't jump in the second; so out goes unlucky Derek . . . Squash now. England's Lancelot Bruce and Norman Kenyon both fell at the semi-final stage in the second leg of the South-East Asian circuit in Singapore yesterday. The final will be contested between Pakistan's Qamar Zaman and Maqsood Ahmed. World number 2 Zaman was startled by Kenyon's fighting start, in which the Englishman won the first two sets, but he pulled himself together and finally won 7–9, 7–9, 9–0, 9–0, 9–2. Maqsood, the number 7 seed, upset third seed Bruce with a stunning performance of stamina and court craft. He won with the loss of only 10 points in 34 minutes, 9–2, 9–2, 9–6 . . . And to close, here's a karate flash, if that's the right word. Scotland won the European karate championship when they defeated former world champions Holland at the Stadium Coubertin in Paris. The Scots beat England in the quarter-finals and Italy in the semi-finals, and now we're moving on . . .

Second part

Joan With us now we have Mike Montgomery, who's going to talk to us about how to prepare for an expedition if you should choose to go by motorcycle . . . that's right, isn't it Mike?

Mike That's right, yes.

Joan You recommend it, do you? I'm afraid I'm the lazy sort who likes to do her exploring from the inside of a car. Do I miss much?

Mike Well . . . I'm a bit biased of course, but I think you do miss a lot, because there's no doubt about it that you do get a totally different experience from travelling by motorbike . . . from what you get in a car. It's a bit like combining the joys of cycling on an ordinary bicycle with the comfort you get in a car. You get all the fresh air, you experience the countryside directly, but on the other hand you don't have to pedal and you're not shut up in a box.

Joan I'll take your word for it, Mike. Suppose we took your advice and went for a long trip on a motorcycle. What would we need to take with us . . .?

Mike Well, above all I believe you've got to be practical and be well prepared for emergencies. I'm a great list-maker, and I've got my checklists divided up under headings like clothing, personal stuff, camping gear, and so on . . .

Joan Shall we start with clothing?

Mike OK. Basics first then. On my checklist I've got two changes of underwear . . . that's both vest and pants.

Joan Which means three complete sets?

Mike Three, yes. One on . . . One set on, one set clean, and one set in reserve. Best wash in the evening so it's dry for the morning, by the way . . . And then, just in case you get any cold weather, one set of long underwear, again both vest and pants, because it can get very cold on a motorbike.

Joan Ugh, I can't stand long underwear.

Mike You would do if you were feeling cold enough, I can tell you . . . As for shirt and trousers, one change only I find is enough. Actually I use army-surplus things from the Army and Navy stores because it's cheap and hard-wearing stuff and it doesn't show the dirt. Doesn't look all that elegant, but who cares?

Joan Yes, I should think it's comfort and hard-wear you go for, isn't it?

Mike Yes . . . For that reason I take one, good, heavy-duty wool sweater – again, I get army surplus ones, even if they are khaki, and a good jacket to keep the wind out.

Joan A jacket? Anorak-style?

Mike	Yes, but be careful, because you need something tougher than a skiing anorak, for example. Leather's good, for that reason . . . it's really tough. In fact that's true for gloves as well . . . that's my next thing – there the best ones are leather, unlined leather, because they prevent sunburn and absorb sweat, and they keep your hands cool.
Joan	Gloves are necessary, are they?
Mike	Oh yes. Otherwise you get blisters . . . your hands really suffer and you can get hurt, you know, on the road . . . stones, grit jumping off the road surface, kicked up by cars in front, catch you on the knuckles or something. Can even make you lose control, and the gloves act as a protection.
Joan	What about special shoes or boots?
Mike	Yes. Cycle boots, good leather ones.
Joan	And a helmet, of course.
Mike	Yes, yes, with a sunshade. And then a good pair of goggles.
Joan	I thought they were going out of fashion, goggles. Don't you have the windscreen instead?
Mike	Well, I don't like windscreens myself because they close you in. They tend to make me feel claustrophobic.
Joan	You like the wind on your face, do you? Any particular kind of goggles.
Mike	I always advise laminated glass, because plastic goggles, however good, do tend to get scratched and distort vision . . . and if also, if I can just add this . . . I think you should be very careful with sunglasses . . . some people use them as a substitute for goggles, but the wind gets behind them and that can be dangerous because sometimes when . . .

Third part

Ginnie	Frank, are you busy, love?
Frank	If I say no, how long will it take me?
Ginnie	It's about the supper party for the drama group.
Frank	In that case I'm *very* busy. Matter of life and death.
Ginnie	Go on, love. Please. You see things like this more clearly, really.
Frank	OK. I'm a sucker for flattery. Fire away.
Ginnie	There's a seating problem.
Frank	What do you mean, a seating problem? There are only six people coming, aren't there?
Ginnie	Only six people, he says. But among those people, Frank love, as in most drama groups, there happen to be at least three people who can't stand the sight of each other at the moment, and if we're going to make this group work, we've got to make sure

	they leave the house as close friends.
Frank	I think I'm playing tennis that evening, actually.
Ginnie	I'll strangle you if you even think of it.
Frank	I really think you're asking for trouble, with this lot.
Ginnie	Too late, anyway. They're coming tomorrow evening.
Frank	OK. You win. Let's make a plan, logically.
Ginnie	I've made four plans already. None of them work.
Frank	Simple, though, isn't it. We've got the vicar and his wife, the mayoress and her husband, and Maggie and Jim.
Ginnie	Now the vicar and the mayoress don't get on, so they've got to be out of each other's range, and the mayoress's husband, Charlie, is deaf on one side, so he's got to go somewhere where he can hear.
Frank	Which side's he deaf on?
Ginnie	The left. I tried him out today.
Frank	Well, let's start with him, shall we? You'll be next to the door, will you? So I'll sit by the window. Let's put him next to you on your left.
Ginnie	On no, you don't. Then he'll only hear me. You have him at your end, on your right. Then he should hear about five people.
Frank	All right. Mine he shall be. Now on his right we must have a woman who is not his wife – which means either Maggie or Florrie, the vicar's wife.
Ginnie	Right. But . . . the vicar's wife speaks in a very low voice, so it'll have to be Maggie.
Frank	Yes, OK. Now that means that Jim and the mayoress must go on the other side.
Ginnie	Yes. Wait a minute. Now, I need to be able to speak to the mayoress . . .
Frank	. . . who should be at the opposite end of the table from the vicar.
Ginnie	So I should have put the mayoress on my right.
Frank	Ahah! Now I can put the vicar on my left then.
Ginnie	With Jim in the middle, yes, that's it. Except that Jim doesn't like the vicar either.
Frank	Too bad. Jim's the organiser of the group anyway, isn't he? He's got to learn how to be diplomatic. Let's leave him there. Then in a quiet moment he can ask the vicar for permission to rehearse in the church hall.
Ginnie	And in another he can ask the mayoress for permission to put the plays on in the town hall.
Frank	Right, and Maggie can keep either the vicar or the mayoress occupied while Jim's doing the asking. She's good at that. I mean, otherwise one or the other will get suspicious.
Ginnie	That's all right then. Now you can go and watch TV . . .

Test 2

First part

Let's have some travel information now. First of all we can tell you on the rail this morning, Southern Rail, we have cancellations on the East Croydon to Clapham Junction line, the 7.57 and 8.28 have been cancelled, the West Croydon to London Bridge line, the 8.07 has been cancelled, the West Croydon to Wimbledon 8.24 service has also been cancelled, and the Wimbledon to West Croydon, the 7.57 and 8.55 services, both of these have been cancelled this morning. No problems . . . which is good news, on the buses or the tube this morning, but some road news . . . at South Morden, South Merton sorry, South Merton, there's been an accident on the B286, Martin Way, involving a tanker and an articulated 32-ton truck . . . well, don't come much bigger than that, do they, I mean what more could you want, a juggernaut and a tanker? . . . anyway, that's on Martin Way, the B286, and there are now long delays between Morden and Raynes Park. On the A24 at Clapham Common South Side, it's subject to delays this morning due to single-file traffic outside the women's hospital . . . The M4 eastbound carriageway will be closed this morning from 9 o'clock onwards between junction 3 at Cranford and junction 1 which is at Chiswick . . . And the A4088, at the junction of Forty Avenue and Barnes Rise. Delays due to gas mains repairs. Not very nice is it? You're tuned to Radio Morden and here is the traffic news as we receive it. Here, just a minute – if you'd like a time-check as you bolt your cornflakes and swig down your breakfast coffee, it's now a quarter-to-eight exactly and drizzling, at least it is here – here are a couple of flashes, one for tube travellers . . . on the District Line, delays of between 5 and 10 minutes between Richmond and Earls Court because of a points failure, don't know where, that's the District Line between Richmond and Earls Court. And the other one's a traffic flash . . . the A2981 south of Chiswick, there are delays at the junction of the A2981 with the A515 just south of Chiswick because of a traffic light failure . . . And one more train flash – I hope this is the lot for this morning – another cancellation, the walking, sorry, I mean Dorking to Waterloo, the 8.05 service from Dorking to Waterloo, cancelled . . . in fact if you want the 8.05 Dorking to Waterloo train you'll be walking, sorry about that one . . . Anyway, let's have a bit of music, shall we? What do you think of this to take your minds of this grey drizzly morning . . .

Second part

Recently people have been growing very interested in the whole subject of the potential of the brain, and in particular the subject of brain rhythms seems to be arousing a lot of interest, perhaps because of the popularity of oriental meditation techniques such as transcendental meditation, in which the rhythms of the brain are slowed down and a great degree of relaxation is achieved. Now in fact, four basic brain rhythms have been observed, and have been given the names of the Greek letters alpha, beta, delta and theta. Let's have a look first at the Beta rhythm, which is measured as having between thirteen and twenty-two cycles per second. Now when our brains are functioning entirely in Beta, we are subject to anger, excitement and tension . . . that is, if you like, that Beta rhythm, which is a rhythm confined to the frontal areas of the brain where complex mental processes take place, is in some way a stress sign, a sign that the brain is overheated, overcharged . . . The rhythm immediately below that is Alpha, which is between eight and twelve cycles per second. Now Alpha is a slower wave and is characterised by a state of alertness and insight, of a calm elation . . . it is a feeling rather as if the brain is working at its best, in what might be described as a state of play, working without worry or anxiety. One of the effects of meditation techniques like transcendental meditation is that Alpha can eventually be achieved at will . . . Below Alpha, in a band that covers from four to seven cycles per second, is the wave called Theta. Theta is apparently connected with mood – it is characterised by a dream-like, almost trance-like state, where, unlike with the Alpha state, there is no state of self-awareness . . . it is rather as if one is drifting off to sleep, losing consciousness. And fourthly, there is the Delta rhythm, of from one to three cycles per second, a very slow wave. This comes in deep sleep, when the brain slows down to its minimum rate. Interestingly enough, in the first years of life Delta waves are predominant, and it is only when the dominant rhythm in a child's brain reaches the level of seven cycles per second, that is, high Theta, at the age of about two years, leaving Delta behind, that the child develops the power of speech . . . It is quite interesting too to note the physiological effects of slowing down the brain rhythms through meditation techniques. One very notable one is the decrease in the heart rate, which goes accompanied by a 20% drop in oxygen consumption. Secondly, there is a general slowing-down of metabolism – that is, the process by which nutritive material is built up into living matter – with a reduced output of carbon dioxide. And thirdly, there is a drastic drop in the lactate level in the blood, and high lactate level is associated with stress. In short, therefore, all three effects suggest that by meditating, people somehow reduce the wear and tear on their bodies, which in turn must make for a more efficient use of their physical capabilities . . .

Third part

Helen   So in fact what you're saying is that some characteristic mistakes are a natural part of the thinking process . . . that they can't be avoided because they arise directly out of the way the mind works?

Stuart Yes, but I should also say that I feel one should always be able to recognise the kinds of common mistake made in everyday thinking.

Helen Which you can do something about . . .

Stuart Yes. Recognising them is the first step. Catching yourself or others in the act, as it were.

Helen Could you give us some examples of the commonest ones?

Stuart Yes. I've narrowed them down to five basic types. The first I call the 'monorail' mistake, which comes when you go from one idea to another without taking into account factors extrinsic to those ideas . . . for example if I say Chinese communism is a good system, so it'd be a good thing for us here too, or . . .

Helen Rather like saying what is good for you must necessarily be good for me . . .

Stuart That's it. Then there's the 'magnitude' mistake?

Helen Magnitude? Getting things out of proportion?

Stuart Yes. The mistake of the type 'If you don't wash the dishes, you can't love me like Jessie loves her husband.' That sort of remark may ignore the great love that might have been shown by the wife's working for 40 hours as a secretary while her househusband looked after the baby and cooked the meals.

Helen Yes, it's very common, that one, I think.

Stuart Yes it is. Then thirdly there's the 'misfit' mistake. Where you fit assumptions together wrongly . . . such as when you say 'you sound like Geraint on the phone and because you have a Welsh accent you must be Geraint'.

Helen Like forcing together jigsaw pieces that don't fit.

Stuart Exactly. Fourthly, there's the arrogant 'must-be' type of mistake, the mistake of the closed mind that resists examining alternative explanations which remain within the bounds of credibility. That's not only a mistake made by scientists, either. As an example, think of . . . 'Dinosaurs all died out within a relatively short period, so someone must have shot the dinosaurs, so we must find out who it was . . .'

Helen That sort of mistake gives you the feeling you want to say 'hold on, hold on, not so fast' . . . an irritation that there is a desire, a lazy desire to treat as certainties things which are not certain at all.

Stuart Yes, in fact the connection between arrogance and laziness is quite strong in thinking . . . However, let's go back over them when I've just given the fifth one a mention. That's the straight 'miss-out' mistake, which involves selecting a solution that covers part of a problem but not the whole of it. A propaganda film may show a magnificent new hospital in a poor country as evidence of progress, while missing out the pictures of children in the next street suffering from disease and malnutrition.

Helen Really, what strikes me about these mistakes in thinking is that we are all prone to make them, aren't we? I mean, one's first reaction may be to say 'oh, how stupid . . . only a fool or someone very careless would think like that' but I see that really they're mistakes that occur with all sorts of people, educated and non-educated alike.

Stuart Oh yes. You can recognise them in the racist, the political terrorist, in religious cults, in extreme patriotism, and in the next-door neighbour who won't speak to you because of something you once said about a friend of his that he didn't like . . .